ARCHETYPES
—— FOR ——
SPIRITUAL
DIRECTION

ARCHETYPES
— FOR —
SPIRITUAL
DIRECTION

DISCOVERING THE
HEROES WITHIN

BRUCE TALLMAN

PAULIST PRESS
New York • Mahwah, NJ

Cover design by Trudi Gershenov
Book design by ediType

Library of Congress Cataloging-in-Publication Data

Tallman, Bruce
    Archetypes for spiritual direction : discovering the heroes within / Bruce Tallman
      p. cm.
    Includes bibliographical references.
    ISBN 0-8091-4358-5 (alk. paper)
    1. Spiritual direction. 2. Archetype (Psychology) I. Title
    BX2350.7.T35 2005
    253.5'2 – dc22

                                 2005003450

Published by Paulist Press
997 Macarthur Boulevard
Mahwah, New Jersey 07430

www.paulistpress.com

Printed and bound in the
United States of America

This book is dedicated to my father
Fredrick Wallace Tallman
(1922–2000)
a Christian hero
whose spirit prevailed over his body
so that he became a great
Sovereign, Warrior, Seer, and Lover

Moyers: In this culture of easy religion, cheaply achieved, it seems to me that we've forgotten that all three of the great religions teach that the trials of the hero's journey are a significant part of life, that there's no reward without renunciation, without paying the price. The Koran says "Do you think that you shall enter the Garden of Bliss without such trials as came to those who passed before you?" And Jesus said in the gospel of Matthew "Small is the gate and narrow is the way which leads to life, and few there are who find it." And the heroes of the Jewish tradition undergo great tests before they arrive at their redemption.

Campbell: If you realize what the real problem is — losing yourself, giving yourself to some higher end, or to another — you realize that this itself is the ultimate trial. When we quit thinking primarily about ourselves and our own self-preservation, we undergo a truly heroic transformation of consciousness.

—Bill Moyers and Joseph Campbell
in *The Power of Myth*, 1988

People seem sometimes to think Christianity is a dear darling, not-to-be-grumpy, not-to-be-impatient, not-to-be-violent life; a sort of wishy-washy sentimental affair. Stuff and nonsense! Christianity is not that. Christianity is an immense warning; a tremendous heroism.

—Baron Friedrich von Hügel (1852–1925)

CONTENTS

PREFACE

Both spiritual guides and spiritual seekers will, I hope, benefit from this book.

While it has been written for spiritual directors and guides and is intended to be an excellent road map for becoming a more fully conscious and proficient guide, people seeking spiritual guidance also can benefit greatly from it through learning about:

- the nature of heroic and antiheroic archetypes and how they help or block spiritual growth

- how to activate the spiritual heroes within, that is, the heroic archetypes

- the impact of heroic and antiheroic spiritual directors and guides upon those under their guidance

- how to identify and benefit from heroic guides and cope with antiheroic ones if there are no other spiritual directors or guides available.

Ultimately, this book is meant to empower, protect, and serve the male and female seekers who so trustingly and vulnerably share their souls with the guide or director in the spiritual counseling relationship.

All of this is extremely important for Christian and other spiritual traditions, because every year hundreds of thousands

of people around the world bare their psyches before spiritual
guides and directors. In a relationship as intimate and powerful
as that of director and directee, great spiritual good or harm can
be done to the soul depending on whether the guide is a hero
or an antihero. Greater understanding of this for both the guide
and seeker is the purpose of this book.

ACKNOWLEDGMENTS

I would first of all like to thank my parents, Fred and Alice Tallman, for pointing me toward God at an early age. My father in particular was concerned that his children receive a solid religious education. He also gave us an example of a person with an indomitable spirit who let nothing stop him and never gave up: although he was a paraplegic and struggled his whole life with this physical handicap, he rose to a very high level in the business world. By the time he retired, he was simultaneously the president of a large insurance company, the senior vice-president of another, and on the board of directors of four others.

Second, I want to acknowledge the wise guidance of Margaret Ferris, CSJ, in the development of this book. From the first time I met Marg to the present day, her calm, balanced, and rational demeanor has caused me to always think of her as a woman of substance, one who exemplifies the Seer archetype. In fact, with four graduate degrees including a doctor of ministry in spiritual direction, Sister Marg was the perfect advisor for me.

I am also grateful for the two years of excellent training in spiritual direction that I received from Bernie Owens, SJ, and Lucia Dubois at the Manresa Jesuit Retreat House in Bloomfield Hills, Michigan.

I want to thank as well all the men involved in the ManKind Project who facilitate the New Warrior Training Adventure. They have not only been responsible for sparking my interest in Jungian archetypes; they have profoundly changed my life.

I should also mention my gratitude to the enlightened leaders in the Diocese of London, Ontario, where I worked as the director of two adult religious education centers for fourteen years. As my employer, they allowed me to take one paid study day per week, which made it possible for me to have a family life while working full-time and completing my doctor of ministry degree in spiritual direction. Ron Pickersgill, a personal friend and also the communications officer for the diocese, deserves a nod of appreciation as well for his help in editing chapter 1.

I am also indebted to the spiritual directors at the Graduate Theological Foundation (affiliated with Oxford University) who read this work originally as a doctoral thesis and voted that it be accepted "with distinction" since it represents, in their words, "a creative new integration of archetypal theory and the ministry of spiritual direction."

I also owe a debt of gratitude to Reverend Lawrence Boadt, publisher and president of Paulist Press, for his patience and helpful suggestions. Paul McMahon, Nancy de Flon, and John Eagleson, my Paulist Press editors, were also extremely helpful.

I would also like to thank all those people with whom I have done spiritual direction in the past four years in my work as a full-time spiritual director. They have profoundly influenced the writing of this book. I have probably gained as much from them spiritually as they gained from me. I hope they will learn a lot by reading this book.

Last but by no means least, I would like to thank my wife, Grace, who has been such a loving and supportive partner of my spiritual direction practice and of the research and writing of this book. Without her patience and understanding, none of this would have been possible.

Chapter One

INTRODUCTION

Four "Coincidences"

Four strange and dramatic coincidences recently happened to me. The first occurred on the Friday before Christmas. I had left my job with the church the previous August, and from August to December I was living my dream of being a full-time spiritual director. I decided to take a break from my spiritual direction practice between Christmas and New Year's Day.

For some reason, the last thing my last directee said to me on the Friday before Christmas was about how she had studied "the hero's journey" in high school. I wanted to ask how the hero's journey related to her own spiritual journey, but our time was up, and so I filed the topic away in my memory banks as something interesting to explore in future sessions.

A few days later, on the Monday before Christmas, I was chauffeuring my daughter around town as she bought some last-minute Christmas gifts. I am not a great shopper at the best of times and particularly dislike the materialistic frenzy surrounding the birth of Christ. At one point I was standing around waiting for her to get through the long lineup at the cash register in a huge chain store. As far as I knew this store sold only clothing, and since I didn't need any clothes, I scanned the store in a desperate attempt to find some relief for my boredom.

I noticed a small rack of videos in one corner of the vast sea of merchandise and struggled through the jostling crowd to make my way over to it. There, before my eyes, was a boxed video set called *The Hero's Journey*! It was narrated by Joseph Campbell, and since I have always been interested in the work of this great thinker and was struck by the coincidence, I bought the set.

The third coincidence occurred on Wednesday, Christmas morning. One of my gifts was a book of poetry from a friend and fellow counselor. In the bottom right-hand corner of the cover was a small painting of a salmon trying to leap up a waterfall. Wondering what that was about, I looked for an explanation, and the back cover said it was a detail from the painting *The Hero's Journey*!

The hero's journey, the hero's journey, the hero's journey! Three times in six days! With this third coincidence I was thunderstruck. As a friend said "These were not *coincidences*, these were *God-incidences*. God has been trying to get your attention and give you a message in a most dramatic way. This was God's special Christmas present to you!"

As I pondered all this between Christmas and New Year's, I had the distinct sense that the message was not meant for me alone. But, I asked myself, what exactly was the message and who exactly was it for? The videos filled in a few more pieces of the puzzle.

THE HERO'S JOURNEY

Joseph Campbell spent his whole life studying the myths that form the foundation of every culture, including our own. He was the greatest mythologist of the twentieth century, and his four-volume book set *The Masks of God* is a classic in the field of mythology. In his most widely read work, *The Hero with a*

Thousand Faces, he wrote that the only myth that he found in every time and every place, the one universal myth, is the myth of the hero's journey.

Around the time when I watched the videos I happened also to be reading Ernest Becker's Pulitzer Prize–winning work *The Denial of Death,* in which he explains that all of us respond so strongly to heroes because everyone secretly wants to be a hero: we all consciously or unconsciously yearn for a heroic life. This, in turn, is because the hero is in some ways the universal *imago Dei,* the image of God, in all of us.

According to Joseph Campbell, there are stages to every hero's journey: preparation for the journey, the journey itself, and the triumphant return. It all starts with a problem, with something wrong in the tribe, nation, realm, kingdom, or queendom. There is usually some overwhelming foe. In traditional children's literature, it is often a dragon who has stolen the princess and whom none of the king's knights can defeat. Then a hero-knight comes along, slays the monster after many trials and tribulations, restores order and well-being to the land, and finally returns to marry the princess.

In the Bible, Goliath arrogantly challenged the Israelite army to send a man to fight him, but no one had the courage to take him on. However, God had been preparing a hero for years, unknown to anyone. David, living as a simple shepherd boy, was learning to protect his flocks by killing lions and bears with his slingshot. Finally, he journeyed to the front lines of the war, and, armed only with his slingshot and his faith, brought about the breathtaking defeat of this impossible foe, and then returned in glory as the new hero of the realm, with the maidens singing, "Saul has killed his thousands, and David his ten thousands."

The same pattern is found everywhere: preparation, journey/
struggle/adventure, and return. The hidden life of Christ for
eighteen years in Nazareth, the triumphs and tribulations of his
three-year ministry throughout Israel, his death, resurrection,
and anticipated return in glory are a paradigm of the hero's
journey.

George Lucas based his original *Star Wars* trilogy on Campbell's work. Luke Skywalker is trained by Yoda to be a Jedi
knight, battles Darth Vader and the Empire, and in the final
film there is the return of the Jedi. In *Lord of the Rings,* Frodo,
the lowly hobbit and unlikeliest of all heroes, lives a simple
life in the shire. Then at Gandalf's prompting he sets off on
an incredible adventure, fights and defeats a seemingly invinci-
ble foe, the Dark Lord Sauron, and then returns home, having
saved all of Middle-Earth. In Harry Potter's struggle with Lord
Voldemort we see the same thing. These are all battles between
good and evil, and they are all wildly popular because they ap-
peal to our deepest instincts. Everyone wants to live like a hero,
to have a life of cosmic significance.

THE FOURTH COINCIDENCE

Now that I better understood the content of the message, I was
left to ponder my sense that it was not intended for me alone.
Who was it for?

Now, as if the coincidence (or God-incidence) of the repe-
tition of *the hero's journey* three times were not enough, just
before Easter a fourth coincidence occurred. One of my directees
had a dream with me and a salmon in it. As soon as he told me
about it, I recalled the salmon in the painting *The Hero's Journey.* God knows I'm a slow learner and obviously didn't want
me to forget the former coincidences.

In the dream, my directee and I were wading up a stream together when we saw a large fish floating belly up in the distance. When we got closer we saw that it had a four-inch gash in its side. As we reached over to pick it up, it suddenly flipped over, displaying all its sparkling red and green colors, and swam away. We realized that the apparently dead fish was a very much alive salmon.

My directee felt that this was a significant and powerful dream, and e-mailed me, wondering how I would interpret it. I went to my library and pulled off the shelf *10,000 Dreams Interpreted*, which said that "in *mythology*(!), the salmon signifies knowledge of other worlds and of otherworldly things. This refers principally to the subconscious" (my italics and exclamation mark). In reference to the stream it noted that "the image of a stream is often quoted as being blessed by divine power." Water represents "the ability to create a new life in response to inner urgings" and "spiritual rebirth — the life-force."

Remembering that Christians represented themselves with the symbol of a fish in the early church, and since it was now almost Easter, I e-mailed him back saying that I thought one interpretation might be that the salmon represented both Christ and him. The gash in the salmon's side represented the crucifixion; the dead fish coming to life represented the resurrection. As spiritual director and directee we were walking together in the flow of the Holy Spirit, which was blessing us both with divine power, healing the subconscious wound of incest that he had suffered at the hands of his mother as a five-year-old boy, and both of us were witnessing his spiritual rebirth and new life in Christ. This interpretation sat well with him, and he said he was greatly encouraged by all of this.

I didn't tell my directee, but the salmon was also very meaningful for me in a completely different way. I pondered why the artist would include a salmon in a painting on the hero's journey? Then it dawned on me: the salmon *is* on the hero's journey.

Born in placid fresh water, the salmon makes its way through streams and rivers to the sea. When it reaches the ocean, it changes into a saltwater fish, swims hundreds of miles away, and grows for about three years. This is the strengthening, the preparation for the heroic struggle. Against all odds, the salmon finds the stream it came from, goes from being a saltwater to a freshwater fish, and not only swims against the current, but also accomplishes the seemingly impossible: it swims *up* waterfalls! The salmon lets nothing stop it and never gives up until it returns to the peaceful waters of its birth, where it spawns.

Since early Christians chose a fish to represent their faith, in many ways it would be appropriate to have a salmon represent Christians today. This might put things into perspective for a lot of believers because Christians today are being called more than ever to swim against the current of our society, particularly, I believe, in its tendency toward ever increasing consumption.

At a deeper level, all spiritually oriented people are being called to fight against the cultural current of making money our Great Idol. Money is the waterfall, the great obstacle for most people to living a truly spiritual life, and we are all called to be heroes, swimming mightily upward against overwhelming odds. Spiritually oriented people cannot ignore or not deal with money; it is an integral part of everyone's reality. It is just a question of priorities: do we make money our number one priority, or do we make God our number one priority? The lives of too many people revolve around money instead of around God.

EVOLUTION, MYSTICISM, AND PLANETARY SALVATION

According to Pierre Teilhard de Chardin, the great twentieth century paleontologist who spent his entire life integrating Christianity and the theory of evolution, the evolutionary process itself is leading us toward the reign of God. God first *involves* (becomes incarnate) in matter and then *evolves* out of it. Planetary evolution moves inexorably from the *geosphere* (matter: rocks and water) to the *biosphere* (life: plants and animals) to the *noosphere* (mind or thought: human beings) and finally to the *theosphere* (spirit: the reign of God).

Each sphere incorporates the previous sphere and goes beyond it. The realm of spirit, the reign of God, incorporates and goes beyond the thought of human beings, who incorporate and go beyond the life of animals and plants, which incorporate and go beyond the matter of rocks and water. The whole astounding process involves organic incarnation and ongoing transcendence or unfolding of the reign of God. God emerges from within everything.

Evolution, in Teilhard's vision, moves in a spiritual direction from matter to life to thought to spirit. Human beings, rather than being simply another branch on the tree of evolution, are central to the whole process, the vital link between life and spirit. However, at the human level there is also freedom of choice and therefore the possibility of sin. Humans, if they are going to be instrumental in taking evolution to the next level, must choose either to love and evolve to a higher level, or to hate, sin, and die.

We can take planetary evolution forward to the place where the Spirit reigns in every heart and the reign of God, the kingdom/queendom of God, is within and among us as fully alive and fully loving human beings, or we can reverse the process by destroying the planet. God is saying once again: "I have set before you life and death.... Choose life" (Deut 30:19).

The problem facing us now, at this critical juncture in the evolutionary process, is that we are living in a materialistic culture in which everything is driven by consumption and money. Michael Crosby, in his *Spirituality of the Beatitudes,* maintains that the major project of Western culture at this time in history is to replace each human being's personal soul with a consumer soul. Since the lifeblood of transnational corporations is money, and since it is these corporations that are running the world at the present time, there are tremendous cultural pressures that are forcing all of us to make consumption, and therefore money, into our main priority in life, that is, our god.

Trevor Turner, a psychiatrist, noted in an article in the April 2003 issue of the *New Internationalist* that he was seeing more and more cases of a new widespread psychiatric disorder. In "I Shop, Therefore I Am" he writes about MSA, Malignant Self-Actualization Syndrome, in which an increasing number of people believe that their only purpose in life is to consume. The Me generation has cocooned, turned inward, and encourages you to focus only on yourself, to the exclusion of all others. Therefore, love becomes impossible and the psyche is dysfunctionally stunted. "Today" Turner writes, "a rising tide of narcissism is spreading like a toxic social algae."

Mary Jo Leddy notes in *Radical Gratitude* that the whole system of Western culture now runs on dissatisfaction or, in other words, ingratitude. Billions of dollars are spent by corporations every year on advertising aimed at making us dissatisfied with the material goods we have so that we constantly crave more, even though the average North American consumes thirty-five times as much as the average person in a developing country. Gratitude, that is, being content with what you have, then becomes a politically radical attitude. Gratitude is countercultural.

Richard Rohr, OFM, one of the most sought-after Catholic speakers and retreat masters in the world today, has compared our greedy culture to passengers partying on a train, unaware that the bridge up ahead is out.

As China, India, and the rest of the developing world get on board the capitalist free-market train, their vast populations present us with the very real danger that overconsumption will take us all over the precipice. This fascination with material goods, this materialism, runs counter to the direction of evolution, leading us back to matter rather than forward toward spirit. There is, however, hope.

All the major religions know how to lead us to enlightenment, to spirit and God-consciousness. What we need now, as the wise and holy rabbi Solomon Schachter once said to me, is to learn how to get enlightened together. Pope John Paul II has been leading the way in this, calling leaders of the world religions to Assisi to pray together. What is needed, however, is for the average person to heed the prophetic words of the Second Vatican Council, which called everyone to be a mystic, that is, to love God with all their heart and to love others as themselves.

Mystics are at the cutting edge of the evolutionary process, the forerunners of the theosphere, the reign of God. They are the heroes of the spiritual life. They spend their early life preparing for the mystic's journey through purgation/purification and the dark night of the senses. Then, by the grace of God, they go on the adventure of illumination, through the dark night of the soul, and finally reach union with God. They then return to teach others about all this.

The role of the spiritual director, or spiritual guide, is first of all to be a mystic himself or herself, and second to lead as many others as possible along the mystical path. We need mystics in abundance.

Fortunately, the Spirit is moving mightily, and thus, according to Spiritual Directors International, about three hundred centers around the world are forming thousands of new spiritual directors every year. This is exactly what the planet needs at this time. Thousands of spiritual directors are called to lead tens of thousands to be spiritual heroes: to go against the current of our culture, to fight the great dragon of idolatrous materialism and, like the salmon, never give up, until everyone is filled with the Spirit and we are all spiritually back on the right evolutionary path toward the reign of God.

No one will be able to lead or guide anyone into spiritual heroism if they are not heroic themselves. Quite simply, no one can serve as any kind of spiritual model or mentor for others if they lead a less than exemplary spiritual life. We all know how damaging clergy sex scandals have been for Roman Catholicism and other churches, but these are just a symptom and the tip of the iceberg of spiritual malaise in our culture.

If Christians in particular, and people in general who claim to be spiritual, do not practice what they preach, if they do not walk their talk, they will have credibility and influence with no one. All of us must strive to become authentic mystics and saints. For our planet to survive, and for the advent of the reign of God, what is needed is for more spiritual people to be genuine spiritual heroes.

So the message of the hero's journey was meant for all spiritually oriented people, and for Christians in particular, since our Western world is Christian in its roots but has now become

Christian in name only. The hero's journey is a wake-up call for all of us.

The period before our conversion, or before we start to take our faith seriously, is our preparation. The journey is our daily and constant struggle against the forces of evil in the world and in ourselves. For Christians, there would be no hope of making it up the waterfall of money, greed, and evil if it was not for the power and grace of the Holy Spirit and Jesus Christ. As Christians we can do all things, even impossible things like swimming up a cultural waterfall, through Christ, who strengthens us. For us, the return is our return to our Father in heaven, our heavenly home and reward for fighting the good fight and never giving up.

REIMAGING MEN AS SPIRITUAL HEROES

Beyond spiritual people in general, and Christians in particular, I believe that men are being called by the evolutionary process to go through a Copernican revolution, to focus on Spirit rather than themselves, and to become spiritual heroes. A subtheme of this book is that, if our world is going to get back on track spiritually, there will have to be a great change in the way men imagine themselves, and understanding archetypes can be very helpful in bringing this about.

If you ask most women, they will tell you that men in general seem to be untrustworthy, immoral, self-centered, and immature, if not downright evil, violent, and dangerous. In Western culture the media largely portrays males as insensitive fools whose main interests are sex, alcohol, and violent contact sports. Unfortunately, many men think of themselves this way as well. Men are, in fact, responsible for most war, violence, crime, and environmental destruction in the world.

There might be more hope for the human race if more men participated in workshops on spirituality, adult religious education courses, prayer groups, retreats, and spiritual direction. However, my own observation after being involved in all of these things over the past twenty years is that women usually outnumber men about four to one, at least in Canada and in my own denomination, the Roman Catholic Church. Father Richard Rohr in his audiotape series *Men and Women* has made a similar estimate of female versus male participation in religious functions on a worldwide basis. This probably applies to other Christian denominations as well. If the world is going to be healed, all churches need to attract more men and help them become spiritual heroes.

In order for males or females to be spiritual heroes, they need to know what heroes are like, how they act, and how this could apply to the spiritual life. The rest of this book is dedicated to this topic. I have chosen to limit my focus to the field of spiritual direction since that is my specialty. We will look at how heroic male and female spiritual directors or guides help directees or seekers become spiritual heroes by modeling healthy spirituality in four forms: Sovereign Director, Warrior Director, Seer Director, and Lover Director. Although we will focus on spiritual direction, these four models could be applied to any aspect of spiritual leadership whether that of rabbis, gurus, imams, priests, deacons, religious, or laity, whether male or female.

HEROIC AND ANTIHEROIC ARCHETYPES FOR WOMEN AND MEN

According to Joseph Campbell and Carl Jung, we all know deep down inside ourselves what heroism is all about, but because we have been living in a cynical and antiheroic age for so long, the knowledge lies buried in our communal memory. Campbell also taught:

> The human psyche is essentially the same all over the world. . . . Out of this common ground have come what Jung has called the archetypes, which are the common ideas of myths. . . . All over the world and at different times of human history, these archetypes, or elementary ideas, have appeared in different costumes.[1]

Jung is generally recognized as one of the greatest psychiatrists of the past century, and his influence is currently greater than ever. Just as one example, Jung's theory of personality types forms the basis of the Myers Briggs Type Indicator, which is widely used as a guide to understanding people in management, education, employment counseling, psychology, and spiritual direction. Worldwide, three million people a year discover their personality type and gain new insight into themselves and the key people in their lives using the Myers Briggs questionnaire.

Jung's deeper but lesser known theory was that beyond personality types there are *archetypes.* One of his seminal ideas was that underneath the subconscious mind discovered by his mentor, Sigmund Freud, there lies another much vaster region, which Jung called the *collective unconscious.* Archetypes form the contents of the collective unconscious.

Archetypes are primordial images, blueprints or power centers that are similar to instincts in that they are hardwired into the brains, nervous systems, and psyches of males and females. According to Jung there is "any amount of literary and historical evidence" that archetypes occur everywhere and in all ages.[2] They have appeared in dreams, myths, legends, religious and nonreligious literature, and historical reality in every culture since the earliest times. Some of the initial archetypes that Jung identified were the Wise Old Man, the Wise Old Woman, and the Shadow (the side of ourselves that we hide, deny, and repress).

As already stated, in *The Hero with a Thousand Faces*, Campbell wrote in 1949 that the myth of the hero is the most truly universal myth or archetype. In 1988, as quoted above, he said that archetypes appear in different costumes, that is, different forms.

Much has been written in recent years about archetypes. Robert Bly's *Iron John: A Book about Men* (1990) and Sam Keen's *Fire In the Belly: On Being a Man* (1991) focus on the male archetypes of King and Warrior. Robert Moore and Douglas Gillette in 1990 wrote a landmark book for the fledgling mythopoetic men's movement: *King, Warrior, Magician, Lover: Rediscovering the Archetypes of the Mature Masculine*. In it they state that "the archetypes of King, Warrior, Magician, and Lover have been increasingly in focus in men's gatherings and publications" and that extensive psychological research has led to the naming of these four archetypes as the four fundamental configurations that, in dynamic relationship, constitute the deep structures of the mature male psyche.[3]

In *Awakening the Heroes Within: Twelve Archetypes to Help Us Find Ourselves and Transform Our World*, published in 1991, Carol S. Pearson writes about the Innocent, Orphan, Warrior, Caregiver, Seeker, Lover, Destroyer, Creator, Ruler, Magician, Sage, and Fool as key archetypes. In 1998 Pearson published a revised version of her seminal book *The Hero Within: Six Archetypes We Live By*, in which she describes the Warrior, Magician, and other archetypes in more depth. In 1997 in *Chakras and Their Archetypes*, Ambika Wauters wrote about the Empress and Emperor, the Warrior, the Lover and the Guru as well as a number of other archetypes. Caroline Myss wrote extensively about archetypes in *Sacred Contracts* in 2001. On her current Web site (www.myss.com) Myss lists seventy different archetypes. Some that are relevant to this book are the Addict, Crone, Patriarch, Matriarch, Priest, Sadist, Tyrant, Martyr, Mystic, Sage, Warrior, Victim, Shaman, Seer, Princess, Masochist, and Lover.

For the purposes of this book, in order to simplify things and provide a solid focus on the key archetypes, I am going to follow the lead of Moore and Gillette in adopting the King, Warrior, Magician, and Lover as four key archetypes, with some modifications in terminology *based on the idea that at the archetypal level of the collective unconscious, the male and female psyche are not all that different.* The Queen, the Amazon, the Crone, and the female Lover are four recognized feminine archetypes that, in the way they function, are similar to the King, Warrior, Magician, and male Lover. *All human beings have masculine and feminine characteristics within them, and when people are fully mature they have integrated the masculine and feminine into their personalities.* For example, the fully mature male knows how to be compassionate, intuitive, and receptive as well as strong, and the fully mature female knows how to be assertive, direct, and decisive as well as loving.

I was on a retreat in 1999 with Bill Kauth, one of the founders of New Warriors. (I will write more about them later.) Although New Warriors since the mid-1980s has focused most of its work on the King, Warrior, Magician, and Lover archetypes, Kauth's retreat was for both men and women, and therefore he referred to the *Sovereign* rather than the *King,* to avoid the awkwardness of constantly referring to the King/Queen. Sovereign could apply to both males and females (e.g., Queen Victoria, who at one point as queen of the British Empire was the most powerful person on earth and ruled over a vast portion of the planet).

I prefer Kauth's approach for a number of other reasons as well. *Sovereign* to me denotes one who has the ultimate authority, responsibility and power, and the Sovereign can thus appear as caesar, maharajah, sultan, tsar, kaiser, prime minister, president, dalai lama, pope, bishop, chief executive officer, or boss. In many countries women are increasingly becoming prime ministers, chief executive officers, and bosses, and *king* is just one cultural, mainly European, manifestation of the Sovereign. Also, the word *king* sounds like a term from a bygone, medieval era.

I personally prefer to use *Seer* rather than *Magician.* To many people, a magician is merely a trickster who entertains people through sleight of hand. *Seer,* on the other hand, conveys more of a sense of eternal wisdom, and therefore corresponds to Jung's original Wise Old Man and also to the Crone or Wise Old Woman. I would use *Sage* rather than Seer, but Sage is generally thought of as male, whereas Seer is more gender neutral. Female warriors are referred to as *Amazons,* but it is becoming more and more common to simply call them *Warriors.* Perhaps *Amazon* sounds too specific to one part of the world.

Thus, I am proposing to call the four foundational archetypes, for men and women, the Sovereign, Warrior, Seer, and Lover.

I am also going to follow Carol S. Pearson's lead and consider the archetypes in their healthy forms to be inner *heroes* or *guides* on the spiritual journey. The archetypes dwell within us and can readily be called upon by various methods to guide us when we need help. I will say more about this later. The inner heroes never appear outwardly as simply Hero, but always in some role such as, for our purposes, Sovereign, Warrior,

Seer, or Lover. I also consider these inner heroes to be *spiritual* heroes because they represent the deepest, finest parts of the human soul.

I am using *hero* here in the same way Pearson does, which is slightly different from the way Moore and Gillette use it. For them, the hero is part of *boy psychology,* that is, the psychology of the immature masculine.[4] The hero in the adolescent boy thinks he is immortal and invulnerable and therefore has to be wounded, usually by the sacred wound of an initiation rite. For example, in some tribal cultures, circumcision is performed by men against the boy's will; he is put into a state of total helplessness and fear, so that he realizes his vulnerability and gains some humility and wisdom. Through this he also learns to trust other males. He learns that they are not there to bring about his worst nightmare, that is, having his penis cut off; they are there to initiate him and love him as a brother. Through this trust of his brothers he knows that he is not alone and becomes a mature man.

The way I am referring to *hero* is as the *mature male* or *mature female,* that is, someone who can be taken as a healthy role model, someone who has been through Moore and Gillette's hero stage already, and who is a fully formed human being who has integrated the masculine and feminine characteristics into his or her psyche.

Moore and Gillette also identified two unhealthy Shadow forms for each healthy archetype: Tyrant and Weakling (King or Sovereign Shadows), Sadist and Masochist (Warrior Shadows), Manipulator and Innocent (Magician or Seer Shadows) and Addict and Impotent (Lover Shadows).[5]

In Jungian thought, there is both the golden Shadow (the positive things about ourselves that we hide, deny, and repress) and the dark Shadow (the negative things about ourselves that we hide, deny, and repress). For our purposes here, the Shadow archetypes will only refer to the negative, antiheroic aspects of the human psyche.

These antiheroic Shadow archetypes are characterized by either complete possession or complete dispossession by the archetype. Complete possession means that individuals think they *are* the archetype rather than the *servant* of the archetype.[6] Complete dispossession means that they think they are totally lacking in any of the archetype's characteristics. Thus, according to Moore and Gillette, the Tyrant has lost all touch with his own mortal and weak humanity and thinks he *is* the King archetype, whereas the Weakling has become overwhelmed by his own human weakness and refuses to take on the responsibility of being King.

I prefer to use *Abdicator* rather than *Weakling*, as Abdicator corresponds more clearly to the negative pole of the Sovereign archetype (as in "abdicate the throne"), and I prefer *Fool* rather than *Innocent*, as Fool corresponds more obviously to the negative pole of the Seer archetype (as in "blind fool").

The Innocents, in Moore and Gillette's thought, are those who take pride in not getting caught as they subtly destroy others. The Innocents rejoice in devious and perverse cleverness, which, to my mind, marks them as Fools. There can be wise Fools, like the medieval court jester, whose role was to keep the king or queen from getting inflated egos, and there can be foolish Fools. I am using Fool in this latter sense, in the biblical sense of Proverbs, that is, as one who lacks common sense or who does not see the truth.

I also think that *Frigid* is better than *Impotent* as a negative pole of the Lover. Impotent denotes a lack of power, whereas Frigid denotes a lack of the warmth we normally ascribe to lovers.

There are thus four archetypal forms that the spiritual Hero wears: the Sovereign, Warrior, Seer, and Lover, and eight archetypal forms of the spiritual Antihero: the Tyrant and Abdicator, the Sadist and Masochist, the Manipulator and Fool, the Addict and Frigid.

I believe these four heroic and eight antiheroic archetypes can subsume most of the archetypes from the writers I listed earlier. For example, the Sovereign archetype could include the Ruler, Emperor, Empress, Patriarch, Matriarch, Queen, and Princess. The Seer (as one who has secret and sacred knowledge) could subsume the Seeker, Guru, Priest, Mystic, Sage, Crone, and Shaman. The Masochist could include the Victim and Martyr, and so on.

In chapter 2 of this book, I will explain in more depth the nature of archetypes, that is, what they are. In chapter 3, I will respond in depth to criticism that the Sovereign and Warrior archetypes perpetuate problematic behavior in the form of domination and violence.

For now, suffice it to say that archetypes are not only tremendously important and powerful; they are also inescapable. They operate in every human being, and because each one has two Shadow forms, we either come under their influence in a conscious, healthy way or are negatively affected by their unhealthy counterparts. For example, anyone in a position of authority over others needs to be aware of, and access in a healthy way, the Sovereign archetype in order to avoid its Shadow counterpart, the Tyrant, from taking over, as happened in the Bible with King Saul, Queen Jezebel, King Herod, and Queen Herodias, and in modern times with Hitler, Stalin, and Mao.

Given the bloodbath of the twentieth century, which has continued to this day, it is understandable that anyone would find it difficult to think of anything positive about the Warrior archetype. However, we don't hesitate to call the police (civic Warriors) if someone is breaking into our home. We know that the police are there to serve and protect us. If our military is healthy, its male and female soldiers function as liberators from oppression, defenders and peacekeepers rather than aggressors. Accessing the Warrior archetype well prevents its Shadow counterpart, the Sadist (or Terrorist) from taking over and destroying civilization. Heroic Warriors keep antiheroic Warriors in check.

Naturally, the most acceptable archetype is the Lover. To give some well-known secular examples from the past and present, the mania generated over movie stars (Marilyn Monroe, Lauren Bacall, Brad Pitt, Richard Gere) and musicians (Frank Sinatra, Elvis, the Beatles, Barbra Streisand, Madonna) attests to the power of the Lover archetype. However, the widespread plague of addiction of all kinds in our society testifies also to the power of the Lover's Shadow side, the Addict. People in any archetypal role cast a kind of spell over us. This explains the endless fascination some people have with presidents (Sovereigns), football heroes (Warriors), and popes (Seers).

The religious traditions of the world are full of heroic archetypal figures. We know of many healthy Sovereign spiritual leaders (Pope John XXIII, the Dalai Lama), Warrior prophets (Mohammed, Dorothy Day, Oscar Romero, Gandhi), Seers (Thomas Aquinas, Teilhard de Chardin, Sri Aurobindo, Mother Teresa of Calcutta), and Lover contemplatives (Teresa of Avila, John of the Cross, Francis of Assisi, Ramakrishna, Rumi, Thomas Merton, Thérèse of Lisieux). And Jesus Christ, for Christians at least, perfectly fulfills all the heroic archetypes: he is the True Sovereign, Warrior, Seer, and Lover.

Some of the heroes and antiheroes, both modern and historical, could be seen as combinations of the twelve archetypes. For example, Saddam Hussein could be seen as a Tyrant-Sadist and Joan of Arc as a Warrior-Seer (*Saint* would be subsumed under *Seer*). Chapters 4 and 5, however, will describe the heroic and antiheroic archetypes in their pure, unmixed state.

Chapters 6 and 7 will then examine how all this applies to spiritual guidance. How might the spiritual director as hero or antihero behave, and what positive and negative effects might this have on the directee in terms of creating directees who are heroes or antiheroes of the spiritual life? What is it like for the directee if the spiritual director is operating out of one of the heroic or antiheroic archetypes?

Chapter 8 will focus on how both directees and spiritual directors can use this knowledge about archetypes to become more enlightened and empowered, that is, more heroic. Readers will learn how to access, activate, and live out of the heroic archetypes. Chapter 9 will conclude with a summary of how heroic and antiheroic spiritual directors do spiritual direction, an exploration of the impact of this on directees, and a discussion of how directees can cope if their present spiritual director is acting out of one or more of the antiheroic Shadow archetypes. Finally we will look at the implications of all this for the field of spiritual direction in general.

As already mentioned, there are also implications for the whole world. Directors and directees need to become exemplary, heroic models of the spiritual life if they are going to swim against the current of violence, greed, and materialism that is already seriously wounding all of God's children, that is, all of us, and that threatens to engulf our whole world. Both individual and planetary salvation may depend on spiritual people becoming spiritual heroes.

Chapter Two

THE NATURE OF ARCHETYPES

This chapter is a bit technical, so the general reader might want to skip it and go to chapter 3. For those readers, suffice it to say that archetypes are powerful components of the human psyche, like instincts, and constantly influence our thoughts, feelings, and behaviors whether we know it or not.

In order to get a deeper understanding of archetypes, we first need to understand the collective unconscious. Jung describes the collective unconscious:

> In addition to our immediate consciousness, which is thoroughly of a personal nature and which we believe to be the only empirical psyche (even if we tack on the personal unconscious as an appendix), there exists a second psychic system of a collective, universal and impersonal nature which is identical in all individuals. This collective unconscious does not develop individually but is inherited. It consists of pre-existent forms, the archetypes, which can only become conscious secondarily and which give definite form to certain psychic contents.[1]

Jung's theory of the archetypes thus came out of his discovery of the collective unconscious, which was a landmark in the history of psychology.

The psyche consists of two complementary spheres: consciousness, and the unconscious mind. The unconscious mind also consists of two parts: the personal unconscious and the collective unconscious. Consciousness floats like a little island on the vast sea of unconsciousness. The ego is the center of the field of consciousness, and it represses or sets aside, in the personal unconscious, contents that are disagreeable to us or that we don't want to focus on at the moment.

The collective unconscious does not contain contents that have been repressed or set aside by our individual ego. Rather its contents come from the human brain structure we inherited through evolution. This structure is common to all human beings, both male and female, and constitutes the foundation of every individual psyche.

Below everything, including the collective unconscious, lies the unfathomable, divine energy out of which the individual psyche and every level of it is differentiated: the collective unconscious, the personal unconscious, the conscious mind, and the ego. Each level of the human psyche is narrower than the one below it. The collective unconscious consists entirely of elements characteristic of the psyche of the human species. It is our primal nature.

Instincts are common to humans and animals and are impersonal, universally distributed, hereditary factors of a motivating and goal-oriented character that often fail to reach consciousness. Instincts are such close analogies to the archetypes that there is good reason to believe that archetypes are the unconscious images of the instincts themselves or patterns of instinctual behavior. Thus, as Jung puts it, "The hypothesis of the collective unconscious is, therefore, no more daring than to assume that there are instincts."[2]

Jung is simply asserting that there are inborn, unconscious, universally present forms that influence our imagination, perception, and thinking and, through these, our external behavior. *Collective* means *universal,* not individual, but since the collective unconscious is universal, that is, found in every human being, its contents, the archetypes, are the same in every person.

Something like *archetype* is expressed in the first pages of the Bible: the *imago Dei* or *God-image* in which all humans are made. A notion similar to *archetypes* is also found in Augustine in the form of platonic *ideas,* which are not themselves formed but are contained in the divine understanding.[3]

Archetypes are like gifts from God, primordial images that are not consciously remembered but are potentialities for responding as our human ancestors did. Humans are thus born with many predispositions for thinking, perceiving, feeling, and acting in specific ways. If an infant's collective unconscious contains a virtual image of the mother, that is, the Mother archetype, the child will quickly perceive and react to its actual mother.

Archetypes are energy flows, like a magnet beneath a sheet of paper: we see iron filings form patterns but we cannot see the magnetic force, only visible evidence of its existence.[4] Archetypes take shape in the contents of dreams, fantasies, fairytales, visions, religions, mythological themes, and symbols rooted in the universal history of humankind. These symbols and motifs transcend the personal sphere, have a determining influence on psychic life as a whole, and have an extremely high energy charge.

We can guide and control the contents of our consciousness by our will, but the unconscious has a continuity and order that is independent of our conscious control. Sometimes an archetype takes hold of an individual in a startling way and deeply moves them, for example, when a normally rational person is seized by the Lover archetype, and falls in love, so that they are caught up, as Jung says, in "boundless fascination, overvaluation and infatuation" with the one they desire.[5]

Jung notes that, "Archetypes were, and still are, living psychic forces that demand to be taken seriously.... Always they were the bringers of protection and salvation and their violation has as its consequence the peril of the soul."[6] Archetypal images and experiences have always formed a central part of all religions, and although they have often been overlaid with dogma, they can still powerfully work wherever faith is alive. However, wherever our overcivilized, rational, and technological world has frozen faith into empty forms, archetypes have "lost their magic power and left us helpless and alone, at the mercy of evil without and within."[7]

Carol Pearson believes there are at least five ways to explain what an archetype is:

1. Religious monotheists could distinguish between the spiritual truth of monotheism and the pluralistic psychological truth of archetypes. Archetypes are like different facets of the one Unnamable God, helping us connect with the eternal and making the great mysteries more accessible.

2. Academics could see archetypes as controlling paradigms or metaphors, invisible patterns in the mind that control how we experience the world.

3. Scientists could view archetypes as being similar to holograms. If you have part of a hologram you can get the whole. The whole is contained in each part, and can pop up anywhere. Jung noticed that the archetypes occurring

in his patients' dreams also occurred in ancient myths as well as contemporary religion and art.

4. Spiritual seekers with a New Age bent could conceive of archetypes as gods and goddesses encoded in the collective unconscious.

5. People interested in human growth and development could understand archetypes as guides or heroes within each of us, which teach us how to live.

In this last view, which Pearson adopts as her own, each archetype has a lesson to teach us, a task for us, and a gift to give us. Since archetypes reside as energy within all people everywhere, they exist both inside and outside the individual human soul. "They live in us, but even more importantly, we live in them."[8]

Other thinkers see the archetypes as the *great stories* men and women in every culture have always lived. They are great stories because people find their identity and fulfillment in living them, and all our strengths, priorities, and values flow from them. To know if you are a Sovereign, Warrior, Seer, or Lover is to know who you are, and are not. It is to know your story, and how you relate to others.[9]

None of us choose our archetype. The archetypes choose us. They are our destiny, fate, or in religious terms our *calling* or vocation. They are gifts of the Spirit of God that are far more basic to life than any specific vocational choice we make when we leave home. Perennial wisdom recognizes that the story we live is fundamentally *given* to us. We are free to choose to cooperate with the archetypal trend that underlies our lives, or disavow it. Cooperation with divine grace makes our burden light and leads to maturity, wholeness, and holiness.[10]

Myths, gods, and goddesses are simply outward projections of psychic contents that reveal the nature of the soul. The great religions of the world set forth the secrets of the soul even more gloriously through temples, sacred writings, and eternal images captured in icons and stained glass that attract and overpower the believer.[11] In Jung's view, archetypes are so powerful that the loss of the power of its archetypal images and symbols signals the loss of power of a religion as a whole.[12]

Chapter Three

IN DEFENSE OF
THE WARRIOR AND SOVEREIGN

As already stated in chapter 1, some people are afraid that focusing on the Sovereign and Warrior archetypes will just perpetuate domination and violence in human relationships. Therefore, before proceeding with a full description of the four heroic archetypes, I want to allay these concerns by addressing misunderstandings about the Warrior. Then I will briefly respond to concerns about the Sovereign. However, before I do that I want to tell a little story about a *vision quest* I went on, and the invaluable lesson God taught me through it.

THE VISION QUEST

For nine years before I left my job in adult religious education, I knew I was being called to be a full-time spiritual director as my life work. The calling was simply there and would not go away. I was also aware that leaving a well-paid and secure job and getting established as a spiritual director in private practice would be an enormous challenge and was something that no one else in our diocese of 440,000 Catholics had ever succeeded in doing. Still, I had been discerning this move for years and knew I was being called to leave my diocesan job and go on this adventure.

I was looking forward to my "Rattlebone" men's group an-
nual canoe trip into the gigantic Algonquin Wilderness Park in
northern Ontario, which was scheduled to occur the day after
I left my job. I thought it would be the perfect transition from
my old job to my new life. However, at the last minute, Bill, our
leader, called to tell me that all the other men had canceled, and
he couldn't make it either. I was greatly disappointed as I knew
I would have had the full support and love of my New Warrior
brothers as I made this dramatic shift in my life.

Bill, a beautiful soul with long, flowing gray hair and buffaloes
and bears tattooed on his arms and chest, has had a lengthy
love affair with native spirituality. Knowing my situation, he
recommended a solo vision quest, which is the First Nations'
version of going on retreat to discern God's will at a crucial
turning point in your journey. Bill said he had done two vision
quests himself in Algonquin; one was a great disaster and the
other was a great blessing.

It sounded both frightening and exhilarating, but I suspected
that God had set all this up, and I knew I needed solitude and
time to contemplate my life and this enormous step I was taking, so I decided to go for it. I was sure I would get some sort
of message from the Great Spirit to sustain me through the
difficult times ahead.

As is God's pattern, the message from the vision quest came
in a totally unexpected way. I was expecting some kind of vision
to appear after four days of being alone in the wilderness. I
had heard of First Nations people having profound experiences
in which they discovered their totem animal, which then gave
them insight into the path they should take. Nothing like that
happened.

The vision quest turned out to be the canoe trip from hell.
After battling for an hour against a strong headwind that

constantly pushed the bow of the canoe to the side, making forward progress almost impossible, I decided to move the packs to give the front of the canoe more ballast. I stood up for a second, the headwind caught me, and I fell in the lake!

This was a great blow to my pride since I had considered myself to be an expert canoeist and had never fallen out of a canoe in my life. I was ready to quit this foolishness and go back to the lodge. However, something prompted me to get back in the canoe and soldier on. I paddled for nine hours into the unrelenting, merciless wind.

When I got to my campsite I discovered that my matches were soaked, so I could not make a fire, my food and clothes were all soaked, the mosquitoes were in a bloodlust frenzy, and I spent two cold and miserable days just trying to survive. I had little time to contemplate anything. However, I had the sweet consolation that at least if the wind kept up, the trip back would be easy, since I would be paddling with the wind at my back.

As fate would have it though, on the last day the winds reversed themselves and were blowing more strongly than ever! After twelve hours of paddling forward, being pushed back, paddling forward, being pushed back, I pulled up to the lodge, got out of the canoe, and collapsed in utter exhaustion on the dock.

As I started the long drive home, I angrily asked, "What was that all about, God? Here I am, leaving a good job and risking everything to pursue my dream of serving you in a deeper and truer way, the way you called me to, and you sent me into four days of hell. And worst of all, I got no message!"

So I drove on, feeling quite sorry for myself and ruminating on Teresa of Avila's retort after the ox cart she was riding in tipped over and she landed in the mud: "Lord, if this is how you treat your friends, no wonder you have so few of them!"

However, after I got over my initial rage and despondency, God's answer slowly started coming to me. The message came more experientially than verbally, for God had succeeded in programming it into every cell and fiber of my aching body, which were all softly whispering to me "never give up."

The long and brutal hours of paddling hopelessly against the mighty and cruel Algonquin wind reminded me of Sir Winston Churchill. The great statesman, after indefatigably leading the British through their darkest and finest hours in the Second World War, was asked to speak at a university convocation.

This man, one of the towering heroes of the twentieth century, gave what is undoubtedly the shortest convocation address ever: seven words. After many long-winded, yawn-inducing speeches by other dignitaries, Churchill was called upon. In his own inimitable style, bulldog face pouting, jaw jutted forward, hands on hips, he stood up and roared at the graduating students: "Never give up . . . never, never . . . give up!"

Then he sat down. Everyone was stunned. Was that all there was? Then, as the message slowly sank in, everyone leapt to their feet and gave him a standing ovation. This was how Britain had survived its greatest struggle.

"Never give up . . . never, never . . . give up!" My viscera, my guts, knew experientially what that meant, and it was this visceral message that God had given me nonverbally and then verbally that kept coming back to me and sustaining me in my first year of struggling to be a full-time spiritual director. The Algonquins were Warriors, and the Algonquin wind was the Great Spirit forcing me to access my inner Warrior for the hard paddle and for the hard road ahead. I had been wrestling with God throughout my vision quest without knowing it.

Much later, another striking coincidence occurred. Almost exactly one year to the day after my vision quest, I was walking down the dusty main road at the Naramata Retreat Center in British Columbia. Naramata has such a legendary reputation for excellence in the United Church of Canada that I felt quite intimidated about going there. So I was very relieved that the retreat I had just facilitated had gone well.

My head was down as I ambled along, and I was lost in thought, when for some reason I looked up. There, by the side of the road, someone had scribbled on a chalkboard: "Never give up ... never, never ... give up! — Winston Churchill."

Stunned that this message should appear in such an unlikely place, and recalling my vision quest, I walked a bit further and saw another sign I had not noticed before. It told the story of the Kokanee Salmon and how the salmon fight against all odds to return from the ocean to this particular stream hundreds of miles away. The hero's journey again!

The Goodness of the Warrior

My point in telling this story is that all of us have within us an inner hero called the Warrior, and this is a noble and good thing. The inner Warrior is what makes someone who is called to be a poet or artist hang in there when they are starving. It is what makes a mother fight for the well-being of her three children when their father suddenly leaves her. It is what made my handicapped father not just survive, but thrive, and become twice the man most nonhandicapped men are.

The Warrior is an essential element of the human race, that part of us that gives us our incredibly resilient spirit and the will and determination to overcome any adversity. It is the inner fighter that causes us to battle against "the slings and arrows of outrageous fortune," as Shakespeare put it. If Winston Churchill had not been such a heroic Warrior, we might now all be living under the rule of antiheroic Warriors, that is, the Nazis.

As Patrick Arnold says, "The perversion of the Warrior archetype is surely the greatest single affliction to plague our planet throughout history," but "ironically, the most effective antidote to this sickness has proved to be none other than the healthy development of the same Warrior archetype."[1] It is only predatory Warriors that need to be kept in check, and it is necessary to have healthy Warriors to do this, to defend the boundaries of civilization against, for example, the Hutus, who killed eight hundred thousand Tutsi men, women, and children with machetes. This was a triumph of the Shadow Warrior, the Sadist.

The problem is not the Warrior archetype per se but rather that too often men function on the lower levels of the archetype. Warriorhood has been reduced today to wrestling, boxing, and the martial arts, and increasingly women are engaging in these activities.

However, Warriors are needed in every arena of life. Academic disciplines have always advanced and avoided stagnation through intellectual battle. And, as Robert Bly points out, more Warriors are needed today to combat the greed and destructiveness of pillaging chief executives, multinational corporations, and unchecked globalization, in which the rich get richer and the poor poorer.[2]

There have appeared, since Bly wrote this, many peaceful (and not so peaceful) Warriors and other activists who have protested corporate domination in many places around the world. Corporations, as they merge, control the media, lobby governments, put power in the hands of fewer and fewer people, and thus take democracy away from all of us. The corporate elite are usually protected by misguided Warriors though, that is, police armed with tear gas, pepper spray, stun guns, and rubber bullets. It is possible for Warriors to become antiheroic by becoming very effective at defending the wrong cause.

Since the Warrior archetype has tremendous drawing power, psychologically unstable men, women, and youth can be attracted to it in an unhealthy way. There have always been male gangs, but today we are seeing the emergence of gangs of female teenagers. In my country, Canada, several young girls have been beaten to death by girl gangs in the past few years. Antiheroic Warriors are also found today in right-wing religious leaders and politicians who declare war on the poor instead of on poverty. As long as deluded people such as terrorists don the mantle of the antiheroic Warrior, responsible human beings must become heroic Warriors to stop them.

Beyond defense however, as Moore and Gillette note, Warrior traditions have been responsible for the advancement of much good in the history of civilization. Zoroastrian Warrior-Kings spread their religion throughout the Near East and thus formed a foundation for Jewish, Christian, and Muslim values.[3]

The Bible proclaims in several places that "the Lord [Yahweh] is a warrior!" (e.g., Exod 15:3). Yahweh was a Warrior-God who fought for the poor Hebrews against their oppression as slaves of the Egyptian establishment. This Warrior-God demanded justice for and from the people of God: they were expected to share their goods and live in equality together and take care of the widow, orphan, and stranger. Moses, the greatest figure of the Hebrew Bible, was a combination Warrior-Seer who liberated the Hebrews and gave the Law to them. King David was a Warrior-Sovereign-Lover who united the Israelite kingdom and gave us the psalms.

Roman Warriors spread Roman law and culture, which formed the basis of the Western judiciary and civilization. European

Warriors enabled missionaries to disseminate Judeo-Christian ideas around the globe in the age of colonization. Warrior energy is universal and vital to the creation, defense, and extension of every civilization. It is essential in world-building, that is, in ensuring the spread of the loftiest morals, character traits, and achievements to all men and women.[4] Courage, self-discipline, self-sacrifice, protecting the weak, and living honorably are central values for the true Warrior.

Knowledge of the healthy Warrior has been lost. The nobility, honor, and chivalry of the Warrior-Knights of medieval Europe disappeared with modern warfare's machine guns, tanks, and nuclear bombs. As war became more technological, the enemy became more nameless and faceless, and the crucial distinctions among *warrior, soldier,* and *murderer* were erased. In the movie *The Last Samurai,* the samurai Warriors, in defending their villages, refused to take up modern weapons like rifles because they involved the shame and cowardice of killing at a distance, and thus dishonored both themselves and their enemies.

The Warrior archetype may be ignored, but as Robert Bly said, there will always be, as part and parcel of male and female nature, a spiritually hopeful and a dangerously hostile part of the human soul, a dovelike part and a toothed part.[5] Since the Warrior archetype will never disappear, the solution is not to eliminate, but to appropriately contain the energy of our wildness, so that it serves all people.

Many women have been victims of the Shadow form of the Warrior, but it is ironic that those who rightly oppose this, if they go too far, can just as easily fall under the power of the Shadow Warrior themselves. In some ways, the feminist movement has been a sustained campaign for recognition of the Amazon (female Warrior) archetype. Women have clearly sent the message that they are just as capable as men in our competitive society. However, some women have overreacted, becoming militant and dogmatic, and have suppressed other archetypes, such as the Lover.

Jane Goodall reported warfare and murder among her chimpanzees, which are 98 percent the same as humans genetically.[6] The Warrior archetype is inherited instinctual energy, and so, like all archetypes, it lives on in spite of our conscious attitudes about it. If repressed, it goes underground into the Shadow and eventually comes out in a more violent form. As Bly puts it, "If a culture does not deal with the Warrior energy — take it in consciously, discipline it, honor it — it will turn up outside in the form of street gangs, wife-beating, drug violence, brutality to children, and aimless murder."[7] Similarly, Moore and Gillette say that, since the Warrior is hardwired into men and women, the question is simply, will we have the Warrior consciously or unconsciously? To be healthy, Warrior energy needs to be acknowledged for its positive qualities and channeled appropriately.

Women welcome healthy marital combat with men who know how to fight well. Good fighting clarifies things if it is done consciously. Unconscious fighting usually just wounds the inner child. Again, as Bly has it, "The adult Warrior inside both men and women, when trained, can receive a blow without sulking or collapsing, knows how to fight for limited goals, keeps the rules of combat in mind, and in general is able to keep the fighting clean and to establish limits."[8]

Warrior energy is necessary in a man or woman's mission in life, whatever it is, and whatever unpleasant labors it may take them through, whether fighting to form a union to secure a just wage, or fighting to get an academic degree. The true Warrior demands that we fight for something beyond our petty self-interest. Idealism is essential to the Warrior archetype, that is, fighting for some larger cause — in our time, survival of our planet, and therefore our species. The enemy is no longer a person, group, or country but our own ignorance, greed, materialism, and fear. The old Warrior fought other men. The new Warrior fights our greatest enemy, our own Shadow. That is what New Warriors is all about.

The Warrior takes dreams, makes goals and plans, and provides the discipline to make them a reality. The Warrior knows how to work as an interdependent equal. The Warrior cares about the common good, justice, and defense of the weak. In ever widening circles, Warriors protect themselves, loved ones, others, cultures, the environment, and finally the planet.

The Warrior emerges when life is in imminent danger, either individually or collectively. Without our inner Warrior any of us would be constantly victimized. The Warrior allows us to be assertive and establish our psychic boundaries so that our rights are not ignored or destroyed. The Warrior archetype is the template for emotional resolve. It marshals our psychic and physical energies to do what must be done, battling onward against all odds.

Disavowal of the healthy Warrior is dangerous because the best psychic choice for men and women opposed to injustice and evil is the healthy Warrior. When there are no healthy Warriors, the unhealthy ones take over, without any mercy. Even the greatest exponents of nonviolence, Gandhi and Martin Luther King Jr., were Warriors, but healthy ones.

THE GOODNESS OF THE SOVEREIGN

A similar response could be made to criticism of the Sovereign archetype. On the one hand, it is criticized because the Sovereign in the form of *King* connotes the patriarchal masculine power of a bygone age.

On the other hand, there have been many healthy kings, such as King David, who ruled with firm justice and attention to religious Law and was genuinely concerned for the welfare of his subjects, particularly the most vulnerable, the widows and orphans. The story of King David taking the handicapped Mephibosheth into the royal household exemplifies this attitude (2 Sam 9:7–9). At its best, *Sovereign* conveys one who rules not just with might but also with right, not just with order but also with mercy. There is a tendency among critics to be so focused on the bad that they throw out the potentially good with it.

In any case, these archetypes are not going to go away. Whether a man or woman is formally recognized as a Sovereign (King or Queen) or not, if they are in any kind of significant leadership role, there will be a necessity to wrestle with the Sovereign archetype. It is far better that we do this consciously, being aware of both the strengths and pitfalls, the glory and shadows of each archetype, rather than unconsciously perpetrating more of the same abuses that humanity has had to suffer so far.

It is particularly when our world is falling apart, as it seems to be doing now, that we all need and long for authentic Warriors and Sovereigns. Men and women need to celebrate genuine power, that is, power combined with wisdom, not only for themselves and their loved ones, but also for the survival of our species in an era of rampant consumerism, environmental destruction, and weapons of mass destruction.

As Moore and Gillette put it, "Our dangerous and unstable world urgently needs mature men and mature women if our race is going to go on."[9] Or as Max Oliva, another leader of men's work, says "Men and women are created to be in a partnership, neither one dominating the other, each using their God-given gifts of gender for the benefit of each other and the redemption of the planet."[10]

Chapter Four

THE HEROIC SOVEREIGN, WARRIOR, SEER, AND LOVER

Before describing in detail the Sovereign, Warrior, Seer, and Lover, and their antiheroic counterparts, some preliminary notes are important.

First of all, in chapters 4 and 5, I am integrating the thinking of Moore and Gillette, Pearson, Oliva, Bly, and others on the archetypes as a foundation for my own speculations in chapters 6 and 7 on how all this applies to spiritual guidance.

Second, while all four of the heroic archetypes are separate and different from each other, they are all equally important. No heroic archetype is superior to the others, and it is all of these archetypes and their qualities in interaction with each other that produces the fully mature person. And they all apply to both men and women.

Archetypes can be lived consciously or unconsciously. People who live them consciously, that is, in a heroic way, have the ability to perceive an archetype's dark side as well as its bright side, and so they can avoid the archetype's Shadow or anti-heroic manifestations. Although one or two archetypes may predominate in their own life, healthy people try to keep them in balance by activating and integrating the other archetypes in their psyche as well. It is important for readers to keep this in mind as they read the following description of the four heroic archetypes so that, as each archetype is presented, it is not taken as one-dimensional or lopsided.

The archetypes presented below are in their ideal form and therefore may seem larger than life, or a little unreal and mythological. This is not surprising since the archetypes come from the collective unconscious, which is also the source of all mythology. It may be hard to imagine such an ideal Sovereign, Warrior, Seer, or Lover and to believe that someone this good could exist. In reality, of course, every man and woman is a mixture of the heroic and antiheroic archetypes in varying degrees.

THE HEROIC SOVEREIGN

The Olympics Organizing Committee, charged with corruption, decided that it needed to improve its image, and therefore asked Nelson Mandela to pose with them and a few South African athletes for a photograph that the committee would then distribute around the world.

Mandela was respected for his wisdom, courage, and integrity before he was imprisoned, and all of these qualities had only grown during the twenty-nine years he was incarcerated for fighting against the injustices of apartheid. Since Mandela was now out of jail and famous world-wide as the revered president of the new postapartheid South Africa, the committee organized the photo op so that Mandela was standing immediately in front of them and the athletes behind them.

However, Mandela asked if they would mind if he reorganized the picture. They agreed, so he asked the athletes their ages. He then put the youngest athletes in the first row, the next youngest in the second row and so on until there were about six rows of athletes. Then he asked the Olympic Committee to stand behind the athletes, and finally he stood behind the committee so that he was at the very back and barely visible — thus giving the world a picture of the heroic Sovereign.

Heroic Sovereigns invert the pyramid of power and put their subjects first and on top, just as Jesus washed the feet of his disciples and just as the pope in one of his titles is called "the servant of the servants of God." The pope is meant to serve the bishops, who are meant to serve the priests, who are meant to serve the laity, who are meant to serve the world.

Heroic Sovereigns create a realm of safety so their subjects might grow. They encourage everyone to develop their gifts. They are not threatened by anyone else's power. The Sovereigns are highly responsible and give a family, institution, or society stability, firmness, and rootedness in the real world and moral principles. They make the hard decisions, in consultation with their advisors, and take us to places we must go in order to survive or grow, even when we would rather not go there.

The Sovereign is the archetype of greatness and spiritual largesse, of self-possession and dignity.[1] The classic Sovereign is benevolent and noble, generative and creative, and bears criticism and defeat with serene composure. Like King Solomon, Sovereigns do not ask for greater wealth or power but for wisdom to know right from wrong so they can govern justly.

Sovereigns have about them an aura of tremendous organization and orderliness. Their presence alone can restore their subjects to rationality, order, and harmony. As Bly says "When the King is present, there is a sacred space free of chaos. The King does not create order; more simply, where he is, there is order."[2]

Traditionally, victorious Sovereigns were believed to be enthroned at the center of the world, from which all creation radiated outward. In fact, *world* here stands for that part of reality organized and ordered by the Sovereign. Outside the boundaries of the Sovereign's influence lies noncreation, chaos, the demonic, and the nonworld.[3] Within those boundaries the subjects are safe and under the Sovereign's protection.

Just as Yahweh in the Bible spoke the Word and created order out of chaos, so Sovereigns create their realm through their decrees and laws. Sovereigns order their realm in a way that promotes harmony and peace, just as Moses organized Jewish life around the Ten Commandments, Christ gave Christians the Sermon on the Mount as guiding principles, and Mohammed, through the revelations given to him by the archangel Gabriel, made the Koran central to Muslim society.

According to Moore and Gillette, the Sovereign has two major functions. First of all, the Sovereign is the organizer, vision-maker, and lawmaker. However, if Sovereigns want their realm to flourish, they must embody the spirit of the law in their own lives, not just decree it. They must live the right order or no one else will. If they do not live rightly the realm will languish, the center will not hold, and rebellion and social, economic, and environmental disaster will follow.

On the other hand, if the Sovereign lives properly, everything in the realm will reflect right order. There will be life, health, prosperity, and justice, and wrongdoing and evil will naturally be driven out.

The second major function of the Sovereign is fertility. The Sovereign is the primary expression of the life-force, the creative energy of the universe. Yahweh had two requirements for the Hebrew kings and patriarchs: to walk in God's ways and to be fruitful and multiply with many wives and children (as Abraham, Isaac, Jacob, and David did). If the Sovereign is sterile, sick, or impotent, the realm will falter.

As part of fertility, Sovereigns know how to create new life in others. They know the realm will be better if others grow. They must be comfortable with their own authority and not be threatened by growth in maturity or power by those around them. The inwardly secure Sovereign takes pleasure in guiding others to fulfillment.

Sovereign energy also expresses itself in blessing. The good Sovereign affirms others by inviting them to an audience at the palace or Vatican or their corner office, getting to know them and bestowing a blessing on them. Being blessed by a king (or priest, bishop, or pope) can have a great impact on people. By her words a queen can bless or curse her subjects psychologically and spiritually. A Sovereign's blessing can bring peace and strength for the journey to the troubled heart. Being valued and praised makes us whole and rightly orders our lives.[4]

The true Sovereign knows that "sacred kingship is not just a political position, but a spiritual vocation, not just a role of power, but a service of responsibility."[5] Heroic Sovereigns think of themselves as accountable to God, the Most High Sovereign above them, and to their lowliest subjects below. They know that, as Sovereigns, they rule as intermediaries between God and their people.

True Sovereigns never consider themselves too great or proud to ask God for help, nor too important to listen to the problems of the poor. They free the lowly and helpless and have compassion for the poor and weak, rescuing them from violence and oppression.

Like God the Father, they are the faithful lover of their people, always present, caring, and providing. Since they care about their subjects, they are trusted by them. The words of the heroic Sovereign are true and sincere. They are leaders embodying integrity and humility.

Sovereigns embody the life principle of the realm. They thrive on seeing their people flourish and on hearing of their accomplishments. They foster creativity and the arts, wisdom, learning, and intellectual endeavors of all sorts, and promote civilization in general.

If their Warrior is integrated within them, Sovereigns act with aggressive might when just order is threatened. They are not concerned with power for its own sake; they simply want to protect those in their care from threats to their well-being. They affirm clearly, calmly, and with authority the human rights of all their subjects. The Sovereign archetype gives a mortal king or queen the power of inner authority. The Sovereign is authoritative, not authoritarian. Integrating the Seer, the Sovereign discerns the truth and acts out of deep knowledge. With the Lover activated, Sovereigns delight in others, maximize praise, and minimize punishment. They radiate vitality and joy.

Heroic Sovereigns are disciplined in performing their duty without complaining. They are normally the guardians of traditional values and conventional morality without being rigid. They encourage devotion to family, friends, institutions, religion, and the world. They value stability and permanence. They create a more just and calm world.

There is hunger for the healthy and true Sovereign. Everyone wants to be in the Sovereign's presence. Everyone wants praise and validation from the Sovereign. The visit to the Sovereign is very emotionally important. The truly great leader's humility expresses itself as empathy and understanding for the challenges facing the ordinary person. Sovereigns' subjects approach them not with dread, but with holy fear, not wanting to offend them in any way because they love them so much.

In treating the heroes within, that is, the archetypes as inner guides for the average person, Carol Pearson brings the archetypal language down to a practical level that everyone can identify with. She sees the goal of the inner Ruler (Sovereign) archetype as the creation of a harmonious and prosperous realm (life) by means of Rulers being peaceful and harmonious inside themselves. The Ruler's main fear is chaos or, in other words, loss of healthy control. The Ruler responds to any problem by finding its constructive use. The task the Ruler or Sovereign archetype calls us to is to take responsibility for our inner and outer lives, and to find ways to express our deeper selves in the world. The Sovereign's gift to us is sovereignty, that is, healthy control over our own lives, and this affects our families, communities, and societies.[6]

Sovereign energy is manifested when parents show concern for the economic and emotional health of their families; when managers, rather than firing difficult employees, work with them to help them be responsible; when any man or woman makes clear decisions for the well-being of the community, nation, or world.

The Sovereign archetype integrates our lives so that we are whole, and our inner and outer lives match. To help the Sovereign keep our internal and external realms healthy, we can activate the Warrior in us to protect our boundaries, access the Lover to keep us compassionate and friendly, and mobilize the Seer to keep us learning and expanding our consciousness. Otherwise, we can get lost in the modern bogs of overbusyness, indifference, or mental stagnation.

The wise Sovereign balances the material and the ecological. Sovereigns have to accept and deal with reality as it is, with the real world of economics and employment. They know that their subjects need gainful work. They also know that each individual deserves a pure environment that promotes healthy physical and emotional development. They believe that the human and environmental can thrive together if just laws are passed that facilitate abundance without waste and pollution. They take steps to ensure that social ethics take precedence over the financial world.

People who have accessed their Sovereign feel in control of their lives. As far as possible, they create their own reality. They know how to take care of themselves and feel comfortable with the physical world of money, work, having a home, and material goods. They can be wealthy, or live simply, based on their own choice. No one but themselves dictates how they will live. They know they can have little and still inspire people with their royal leadership, as Gandhi proved.

Sovereigns know that evil is real. They have their feet on the ground. They don't allow themselves the illusion of thinking that they can let their mind wander among the clouds while enemies threaten their people. They know how to play power politics when necessary, but their hearts are unsullied. They know how to run with wolves, be wise as serpents, and innocent as doves, all at the same time. Sovereigns also know their own Shadow and have the humility to see when they are becoming dogmatic Tyrants.[7]

Heroic Sovereigns either access their inner Seer or listen carefully to the Seers in their life, their advisors. With their inner or outer Seers, Sovereigns develop a vision for their realm, make plans that match the vision, and then make their plans a reality. They then hold themselves accountable for the success of the plan. If there is disorder, they blame themselves and take responsibility. They do not destroy others to hide their own failure.

True Sovereigns know their own limits and those of others. They don't expect the impossible and they have no time for self-deception. They know their power is limited by human weakness, lack of wealth, and mortality. Defeat is treated as a learning experience, so mistakes are not compounded. They have no desire to lord it over others but rather try to work *with* them. Any desire for absolute power is overcome as they accept their own fallibility and recognize the Sovereign in others.

Sovereigns are about inclusivity not exclusivity. They try to draw all the people in to use their unique gifts for the good of the whole realm. Since people are so different, this can result in conflict, but the Sovereign knows that conflict can produce creative results. Sovereigns do not scapegoat the weak nor get rid of their opponents. They take problem people in, even if it involves self-sacrifice on their part.

Sovereigns try to rule from their true self, the deepest and wisest recesses of their being. They listen not just to their inner and outer Seers, but also to God. As they surrender all self-serving and self-indulgence to God, the One True Sovereign, they find that they become truly empowered and in harmony with the universe, and they spontaneously live right order so that ruling with integrity and justice happens naturally.

In order to understand the true Sovereign better, Christians, or people of any faith, can learn from Jesus Christ. In church, Christians affirm that Christ is priest (Seer), prophet (spiritual Warrior), and king (Sovereign), not realizing that they are using archetypes to describe him. Indeed, for Christians, Christ is the True Sovereign, Warrior, Seer, and Lover all in one, the perfect fulfillment of all the archetypes.

Christ, as true Sovereign, walked away when people wanted to make him a political king. This was a replay of his third temptation in the desert: to rule the world by absolute power. Jesus ignored the adulation and political agenda others had for him, never exploited his authority for personal gain, and never asked his followers to abandon their rationality, responsibility, and autonomy. He told his disciples to become like little children, instead of seeking positions of power. He commanded his followers to avoid the pagan style of authority, that is, lording it over people. He encouraged them to serve, not intimidate, the community.

Jesus blessed his disciples by entrusting to them his teaching, and by showing confidence in their ability to preach the good news. He used attraction rather than force, elicited love not fear, led people by example rather than dominating them. Neither did Jesus dither, befuddle people, avoid thorny issues, or make compromises. He was no Abdicator. He stood up against the forces of political and religious expediency in contrast to Pilate, the false Sovereign, who let the crowds and religious leaders manipulate him. The authority of Jesus was direct and clear. He commanded and ruled with love. He asked of his followers nothing that he did not do himself: to love their neighbors as themselves and to love God totally.

Jesus exhibited the marks of the true Sovereign, that is, internal nobility and psychic greatness, even when all the trappings of institutional power collapsed. When Jesus was stripped of everything, his inner Sovereign shone forth. The true test of inner sovereignty comes not from conquest or riches but from disaster. The true Sovereign shows royal greatness in the midst of defeat. Christ endured a series of disasters nobly: he was unjustly convicted by the courts, deserted by friends, mocked by cowards, rejected by religious authority, executed by soldiers, and felt abandoned by God. Yet he remained a true Sovereign: forgiving, self-possessed, and great of spirit. He demonstrated decisively that inner royalty is completely unrelated to external trappings. The true Sovereign can be found among those most despised by ordinary human beings.

To sum up, Sovereigns are about blessing, generativity (creating new life and growth in others), ordering, and organizing. Sovereigns provide a center for the realm that holds things together. They create the realm by laws and decrees and then embody the spirit of the law in themselves. They live the right order and thus create stability and balance, a realm of safety, harmony, and peace. The Sovereign archetype is the archetype of spiritual greatness, nobility, responsibility, and service. Sovereigns have authority but are not authoritarian. Their sovereignty is about having just the right amount of healthy control. They do not lord it over others. They are humble and know their own limits. Sovereigns are benevolent and rule with love, compassion, and understanding. Sovereigns are mediators between God and the poor. They seek justice while creating prosperity. The Sovereign is a protector and provider for the weak. The Sovereign is a realist, not an idealist, and walks in the ways of God.

THE HEROIC WARRIOR

If our cause is a mighty one, and surely peace on earth in these days is the great issue of the day, and if we are opposing the powers of darkness, of nothingness, of destruction, and we are working on the side of light and life, then surely we must use our greatest weapons — the life forces that are in each one of us. To stand on the side of life we must give up our own lives.   — Dorothy Day

The goal of heroic Warriors, such as Dorothy Day, is not to totally destroy their enemies, but to create new life for everyone through struggling and never giving up. In bygone days, knights were chivalrous Warrior-protectors. The knight's code of honor at King Arthur's legendary Round Table focused on personal honor, noble restraint, magnanimity to defeated rivals, and humility about one's deeds.[8]

According to Carol Pearson, the Warriors' main fear is powerlessness and ineptitude. Their response to a dragon/problem is to slay it if necessary or convert it if possible. Their task is high-level assertiveness, fighting for what really matters. Their gifts are courage, discipline, and skill.[9]

Moore and Gillette clearly delineate the nature of the Warrior, so I will summarize their thought on this. The Warrior path is a total way of life — the Warrior's Dharma, Tao, or Way. In this view, assertiveness is a stance toward life that energizes us to take the offensive against life's problems. Knowing how much assertiveness is appropriate under changing circumstances requires clear thinking and discernment. Therefore, the Warrior is always alert. Warriors cannot afford to sleep through life. They know how to focus their mind and body to get results. Samurai call this *being mindful.*

Warriors are strategists and tacticians. They know what they want, and how to get it. Through mental clarity, Warriors realistically assess the strength, skill, limitations, and weaknesses of themselves and their enemies. The skillful Warrior is flexible and shifts tactics if an approach is not working. Warriors challenge with sharpness and self-confidence. They live in the *now* with a constant awareness of their own possibly imminent death. Therefore, they live with a vitality and intensity unknown to others, and make every action count.

There is no time for anything but meaningful acts, if death is the Warrior's constant companion. Thus, Warriors do not hesitate. They take immediate decisive action and engage life. To think *too much* or to doubt is to lose the battle. Their movements are unconscious reflex actions trained for with enormous self-discipline. "The Warrior energy is concerned with skill, power and accuracy, and with control, both inner and outer, psychological and physical. The Warrior energy is concerned with training men *to be all that they can be* in their thoughts, feelings, speech and actions."[10]

Warriors exhibit tremendous control of themselves and their attitudes. Their mental focus is constantly on being accountable, courageous, and unconquerable, even in captivity or defeat. Discipline and goal-orientation allow them to ignore pain. They lead sacrificial lives, taking suffering and hardship in their stride.

Warriors always have their eyes on some prize greater than themselves. Some cause, person, or ideal has captured their hearts, and they will follow their fierce loyalty all the way to death if necessary. They are willing to throw themselves between the president and an assassin's bullets, if it will save democracy. Dominated by their overarching concern, whatever it is, they are willing to let go of personal interests and people that are less important to them than their cause.

Wherever there is sustained injustice or evil on a grand scale, Warriors will rise up to overthrow the oppressor. Warrior energy is at the heart of every social revolution because the true Warrior is always on the side of the disadvantaged. They are Robin Hood, stealing from the unjust rich to give to the poor.

Warriors are very discriminating when it comes to destruction. They never engage in unnecessary harm or excessive force. They destroy only to achieve some greater good: their overarching commitment. They cut off only what needs to die in order for a higher value to emerge. Most of the time, the police simply defend the boundaries of civilization. Occasionally, they become Elliot Ness and the Untouchables fighting Al Capone and the Mafia to protect the citizenry of Chicago. Or ordinary women rise up to form the Temperance League, or Mothers Against Drunk Driving (M.A.D.D.), to protect families against the ravages of alcohol.

Warriors of every stripe eliminate corruption, injustice, obsolete forms of government, ossified religious structures, corporate hierarchies that hamper performance, unfulfilling jobs and lifestyles, and irrevocably dead marriages. In destroying what no longer serves people, Warriors often build new civilizations and new business, artistic, and spiritual ventures for humanity.

Religious reformations are often fueled by Seers whose spiritual insight leads them to become holy Warriors for God. For example, John of the Cross, a Seer and Lover of God, became a Warrior trying to reform the Carmelite order and underwent torture and imprisonment for his cause. Martin Luther stood alone for what he believed was the truth, against the mighty bastion of the Roman Catholic Church. And Mohammed's belief in the supremacy of Allah caused him to wage war against polytheism. Naturally, there is always the danger of the Shadow Warrior, the Sadist, taking over religion and promoting witch hunts and Inquisitions in the name of God, but we will treat that later.

True Warriors can think clearly and objectively because they have the ability to be emotionally detached. Their focus on the task rather than on people allows them to be coolheaded in the thick of tension and stress. They dispassionately size up a situation and then act with vigor, efficiency, and measured force. In war they are not intentionally cruel, but must separate themselves from their enemies, whether internal or external. They must keep their personal ego needs and wishes and negative emotions such as fear and anger under lock and key. They never kill simply out of uncontrolled rage, as in domestic violence or drive-by shootings.

There is a story of a samurai who was locked in a fight to the death with the strongest henchman of an opium dealer, who for decades had been destroying the will of the people in a large Japanese village. The opium dealer had immense wealth and power and had hired a gang of toughs to do away with the samurai, the opium dealer's last barrier to absolute power over the masses. The samurai, however, defeated all the thugs with his sword. The opium dealer then hired the most excellent swordsman in the land to do in the samurai. The swordsman, although legendary in the skill of his craft, had never fought a samurai. They battled for hours, exchanging one ringing blow after another on their swords. Finally, the swordsman became exhausted, and when it was apparent that he was going to die at the hands of the samurai, he got in a final blow by insulting the samurai's ancestors. The samurai dropped his sword and walked away from the fight. The samurai's disciples were shocked by his apparent cowardice. However, when they asked him later why he walked away, the samurai said that it was because he did not want to kill his opponent out of anger. A samurai's motives must be purely for the cause, without any self-interest or personal ego-involvement.

Warriors are indefatigable in persistence, but if they are not tempered and modified by the other archetypes, their simpleminded devotion to their cause to the exclusion of everything and everyone else can cause problems, particularly with family members who don't have the same commitment. Their detachment can make them emotionally unreachable.

Warriors need the Sovereign to help them go beyond courage and discipline in dispatching what blocks life. The Sovereign can help the Warrior become actually life-affirming and life-giving, a mentor and model to the young. Accessing the Seer allows Warriors to bring divine perspective to their work, so that, while still dispassionately discharging their obligations, they do so with a sense of compassion for everything frail and mortal. Lover energy can keep Warriors connected to spouses, children, and friends as they relentlessly fulfill their mandate.

Normally, a Warrior serves and defends a Sovereign with fierce allegiance, knowing that the whole realm will be destroyed if the Sovereign is taken or killed. Thus, the Knights of the Round Table defended King Arthur and the samurai protected the Japanese emperor. Sovereigns, in consultation with their Seers, decide which battles the Warrior will engage. A Sovereign obsessed with greed and power is transformed into a Tyrant and similarly transforms the Warrior into a mercenary, a hired killer. Under a healthy Sovereign, and in service to a just cause, Warriors are willing to undergo any kind of hardship. All their senses are on alert and they are physiologically ready to cope with fatigue, hunger, torture, or whatever happens to them.

Our inner Warrior can teach us how to stand up for ourselves and our cause, whether it is in the political arena, at work, at a university, or in relationships with our significant others. None of these relationships work well without clean, healthy fighting. If people are passive, nothing gets resolved. If they are aggressive, politics descends to mudslinging and marriage to name-calling. The inner Warrior teaches us the middle path of assertiveness: we learn to speak the truth with love, to get our needs met while treating our opponent with dignity and respect, to be honest but tactful.

If we have no inner Warrior to defend us, others may feel they can freely cross our boundaries. Particularly since we live in North America, which is a Shadow Warrior culture based on winning at any cost and therefore begets all kinds of subtle and overt violence, we need to protect our boundaries. We cannot let every devious or aggressive salesperson, telemarketer, or advertiser into our space if we want to maintain our sanity.

Warriors conserve their energy so they do not flame out before reaching their goal. They are not more assertive than is appropriate. They decline challenges they believe will not bear fruit. They take the long view and maintain a pace of action such that they can call upon extra reserves of strength when the road gets tough.

Warriors do not fear disapproval or care about others' opinions of them. Their main concern is integrity with themselves, to live according to their own beliefs and ideals. They follow their own conscience and ethical standards, no matter what external pressures are brought to bear, or how different from others they have to be. Warriors set goals according to their own values and will defend them no matter what the cost. They live by the motto: "If you do not stand for something, you will fall for everything."

The Warrior has two major defenses: secrecy and strategic retreat.[11] Secrecy is about camouflage and knowing we should never enter a battle until we are prepared for it. It is about not raising issues until we know it is worth the risk, and until we are ready to protect ourselves. Strategic retreat is about smart fighting. It means backing off when we are overwhelmed in order to nurse our wounds, heal, rebuild our strength, learn new combat skills, think over how to attack, bide our time, and wait for the right opening.

Smart Warriors have the wisdom to know when and where to fight. They control the combat and fight according to their battle plan. They identify likely opponents, obstacles, and challenges, and devise ways to overcome them. After listening to advisors, they may adjust their strategy, but they keep their goals clearly in mind and convince others to support their goals. They know what they want and are willing to fight assertively for it, telling others clearly and respectfully what their desires are.

Warriors engage in combat only when all other options have been exhausted. Most of their battles are fought with their wits, out of sight of anyone. They know that their defeat is always a real possibility, so when it happens in spite of their best efforts to prevent it, they are not shocked or dismayed but try to salvage what they can by learning from defeat.

If Warriors win, they help their opponents save face by treating them with dignity. They try to build peace, not make war. They try to avoid actual battle by negotiating with their opponent beforehand, using a win/win model of conflict resolution. The true Warrior prefers peace but will not back down from conflict if necessary.

Warriors thrive on achieving difficult goals. They welcome competition and strive for independence for themselves and others. In short, they can do well in our Warrior culture, and at the same time improve it. The true Warrior sees beyond the status quo, dreams of a world of excellence, and struggles to bring it about. Since Warriors are frequently pacifists and social revolutionaries, they can bring peace and justice to a society or even internationally.

Many people have taken to the streets in Seattle, Quebec City, Genoa, and other places in peaceful Warrior protest against unaccountable global corporations that put profits before people and the environment. They have bravely faced riot police, sometimes even getting killed in the process.

On the spiritual quest we must use Warrior energy, courage, wisdom, self-discipline, and skill to face our inner demons and dark Shadows, the enemies within. This is the true *jihad*, the true holy war, according to Islam. This is what the ManKind

Project and New Warriors promote: men rediscovering the sacred masculine by facing their Shadow, no matter how painful. Healthy Warriors work through their pain: their emotions of fear, grief, anger, bitterness, and despair. They do not deny or simply endure suffering, they integrate it into their lives. They integrate their anger and express it appropriately and justly, as Jesus did when he cleansed the temple of moneychangers.

Jesus and the Buddha were spiritual Warriors who withstood every temptation. Yahweh in Judaism and Allah in Islam are Warrior-Gods. Islam as a whole is built on healthy Warrior energy, that is, striving for excellence, justice, and peace. Mohammed and his followers fought an actual holy war against the unbelievers of the surrounding polytheistic tribes.

In Christianity, the holy war is essentially between Christ, leading the forces of light, and Satan, leading the forces of chaos and darkness, as Ignatius of Loyola so graphically depicted in his *Spiritual Exercises.* Warrior energy also has been present in Christianity in mythological heavenly places, in the form of the archangel Michael, forever battling the rebel angels.

The Jesuits were Warriors who practiced self-negation in their cause of carrying God's message into the most hostile situations. Often their very lives were at stake, whether in Henry VIII's England, where Catholic priests were being executed, or among aboriginal tribes in the Amazon rainforests, or in Canada where many Jesuits were tortured to death by the Iroquois. They modeled themselves after Jesus, who showed Warrior courage in setting his face like flint toward Jerusalem, knowing that death awaited him there.

In summary the heroic Warrior archetype is about single-minded focus on some commitment, cause, or ideal that is larger than one's self, such as freedom, or equal rights for the marginalized. The healthy Warrior exhibits great discipline, courage, self-control, and perseverance out of a sense of loyalty to this ideal. Warriors are willing to sacrifice and suffer hardship for what they believe in. They fight for the right against corruption and injustice of all kinds, cutting off and killing only what needs to die in order for new life to come. Their emotional detachment allows them to think clearly and to accurately assess situations. Warriors have a great deal of energy and passion for their cause, while at the same time being paradoxically objective and dispassionate. They are alert in the *now*, flexible strategists who shift tactics if something is not working and know when to fight, when to strategically retreat, and when to use secrecy. Under the guidance of a Sovereign, they mark off the boundaries and then defend them with great skill. Warriors know their greatest enemy is their own ego and its inner demons of fear, grief, anger, and despair.

The Heroic Seer

The most difficult archetype for Westerners to understand is the Seer. Our left-brained, rational, scientific culture has difficulty grasping what the right-brained, intuitive, magical Seer is all about. Yet Moses, Jesus, and Mohammed, the founders of the great religions of Judaism, Christianity, and Islam, upon which most of Western culture was built, were all Seers who did miraculous, seemingly magical things. There is the story of Moses throwing down his staff, which turned into a snake and ate the snakes formed from the staffs of Pharaoh's magicians. There are the stories of Jesus multiplying the loaves and fishes, and of Mohammed's night flight to heaven. The golden Dome of the Rock mosque in Jerusalem marks the spot where Mohammed's horse allegedly took off in flight.

Magic was originally associated with *magi* — sages or holy men, men of profound secret knowledge, wisdom, and depth. Paradoxically, science and technology have developed to such an extent that it is now scientists and "techies" who do wondrous, seemingly magical things. As Joseph Campbell noted, science and mythology no longer conflict because:

> Science is breaking through now into the mystery dimensions. It's pushed itself into the sphere the myth is talking about...the interface between what can be known and what is never to be discovered because it is a mystery that transcends all human research.... That's the reason we speak of the divine. There's a transcendent energy source.[12]

The shaman, medicine man or medicine woman, priest or priestess, healer, doctor, desert father or mother, mystic, mythologist, philosopher, physicist, computer wizard, psychologist, therapist, and counselor of every stripe (including spiritual directors!) all operate in the Seer realm.

The goal of the Seer is the transformation of lesser into better realities. Seers fear that evil, that is, transformation in a negative direction, will overtake those they are trying to help. The Seers' response to a dragon/problem is to transform or heal it. Their task is alignment with the true nature of the cosmos, and their gift is wisdom.[13]

The Seer is the ritual elder, male or female, who knows and guides the process of transformation and ritual initiation. The male Seer traditionally initiated young boys into mature manhood. Since there is little of this initiation in our culture, we live in an age of personal and gender identity chaos, boys never become mature men, even though they inhabit a man's body, and patriarchy (boy psychology — the immature masculine) continues to rule us.[14]

The true Seer has the interests of people and the planet in mind. Robert Bly, Bill Kauth, Sam Keen, Robert Moore, and Richard Rohr are Seers in the men's movement; through retreats they initiate men into deep masculinity using poetry, story, myth, and religion. They take us beyond male domination and the denial of the feminine in men, which have resulted in the male sins of oppression of women, persecution of homosexuals, and exploitation of the Earth.[15]

True Seers, if initiating someone, use their gifts prudently and are always mindful of the capacity of the receiver to integrate the new knowledge. Truth can be damaging if the recipient is not ready to hear it, or if it is presented in a callous way. Seers know the enormous power of the archetype and first of all insulate us from it; then they help us let out its immense energy a bit at a time, at a pace we can handle.

Seers are themselves initiates into secret and hidden knowledge and training of all kinds. In modern times Einstein, Jung, Madame Curie, Joseph Campbell, Bill Gates, and others saw into the depths of things and initiated all of us into new and wonderful realms.

Seers in ancient cultures always had great power. They were the sage or crone, prophet or prophetess, who could see into the future and warn the people about what was coming, for example, a harsh winter or invading army. The Seers knew the ways of the four worlds: plants, animals; humans, and spirits. They were sought out for spiritual advice, for healing with herbs, to bless the harvest or the hunt. They could also bless or curse your life.

In some African tribes, if the witch doctor cursed you it meant certain death. The psychic power of archetypes is overwhelming. There are stories from years ago of people going insane when they were excommunicated by Catholic priests. Aboriginals everywhere held the medicine man or medicine woman in awe and fear, and he or she was the chief's main advisor. The health and survival of the tribe depended on the Seer as much as on the Sovereign (chief) and Warriors (braves).

The Seer archetype helps us to live in integrity with our soul's purpose. When we flow with what our intuition tells us, things come easily, the right people and resources show up in our lives, and *synchronicity* happens, that is, the seemingly miraculous coordination of events. When we are not at one with our life direction, things start to fall apart.

Any one of us can use shamanic methods to plunge into our right brain and collective unconscious: meditation, drumming, trance-dancing, extended prayer. These other worlds or altered states can give us new energy and purpose. Through guided fantasy, hypnosis, or dream work, we might imagine a dialogue with our inner Seer and gain new wisdom we can apply to everyday problems. Most people may not believe it, but extrasensory perception is a very real possibility for all of us. To be psychic, all we have to do is trust whatever inner voice or inner knowledge seems trustworthy.[16]

The Warrior's main gift is action, and the Seer's main gift is thinking. Seers exhibit grace under pressure since they have the capacity to access deep and unshakeable eternal truths. Seers see the big picture and therefore are not thrown into chaos when a crisis strikes. It is the Seer in the Warrior that allows Warriors to make complex decisions with rational detachment. The Seer is the archetype of thoughtfulness, reflection, expanded consciousness, and insight.[17]

All four archetypes need balancing by the other three. Standing alone, none of them forms the fully mature human being. If mixed with the Sovereign's benevolence, the Lover's harmony, and the Warrior's courage, Seers can use their secret knowledge to serve everyone.[18]

The Seer is open to the many ways God speaks to us, internally and externally. Seer energy helps us make the right decisions for our external life, and the voice within points us to inner peace. The Seer's intuitive right brain draws upon the vast storehouse of the personal and collective unconscious. Thus, Seers often know instinctively what to do, without being able to pinpoint *how* they know. The Seer just knows. Seers guide, by example, to a greater integration of the masculine and feminine, the rational and the intuitive, courage and commitment. They show us the way of love, respect, patience, listening, hope, and surrender to God.

The spiritual Seer is in touch with the harmony of the natural world and respects how every creature can point us to God. As the archetype of awareness, Seer energy teaches us to awaken to the miraculous and to the unfathomable suffering, beauty, and grandeur of life. It allows us to understand the hopes and fears of others and teaches us about their motives, moods, dreams, and imaginings. The Seer helps us to heal, to uncover the unconscious, to bring to consciousness forgotten hurtful memories and idolatrous identifications that trap us in negativity or sin.[19] The Seer creates sacred spaces such as sweat lodges and temples that promote purification and healing and free us to be our true self.

Most of us have at least some internalized abusive voices from our past that hold us down and limit our possibilities. Getting in touch with our inner Seer can help us to know who we really are. The Seer helps us to reimagine ourselves, encouraging us to substitute "I am wise and helpful" for "I am worthless," to replace "I am no good" with "I am competent and lovable."

The Seer empowers a child by naming the child "energetic" or "imaginative" rather than "hyperactive." The Seer may rename an "old man" as an "elder" which gives him an entirely new role in the community, someone who people go to for wise counsel.

Anyone who takes on and takes in someone else's emotional or physical pain is a type of Seer, a healer who unblocks the person's *chi*, their inner energy, and lets this healing energy flow again. Massage therapists, nurses, doctors, chiropractors, and reiki masters have secret knowledge about our body's inner wisdom and release it so that illness can be overcome. Psychotherapists of all kinds help us release our emotional demons. Buddhists act as heroic Seers when, out of compassion, they absorb someone else's negativism and transform the person's pain by sending back concentric and ever expanding ripples of unconditional love.

Seers know the power of rituals and use them for many positive purposes. They know how to employ rituals to help people let go of negative habits, relationships, and attachments. Rituals can be instrumental in changing our consciousness or our identity, as when a Jewish boy becomes a man at his bar mitzvah, or an adult is baptized as a Christian. Transition from the old ways or old life to the new can be effected through ritual process.

Seers first of all heal themselves. They do this by practicing various rituals that connect them on a deep level to their heart and the cosmic Way, Logos, or Tao. These rituals, including prayer and contemplation, unify the disparate parts of their souls so that their Persona (the way they want others to see them) and their Shadow (what they hide from others) are integrated, and conscious and subconscious become one.

Aligning their heart and soul with God and with their work makes it possible for Seers to heal others. Not all Seers are healers, but all learn to awaken their inner Seer by listening to their intuition, whether it is an inner voice, feeling, or vision.[20] Some go beyond intuition and develop extrasensory perception or other paranormal powers.

Heroic Seers always befriend death. Death becomes their main friend and advisor, always reminding Seers to keep their inner eyes, the eyes of the heart, firmly fixed on what is eternal. This allows Seers to avoid temporal temptations such as fame or money. The Eternal One helps them swim against the current, to leap up the waterfall of transient, shortsighted ends that our urgent, frantic, instant-gratification world presents them with on a daily basis.

Seers recognize their Shadow, their capacity to do evil, and befriend it as well. Befriending death and befriending the Shadow disempowers these two seemingly negative enemies of the human soul. Death and the Shadow can cause us to do evil only if they are denied, for then they control us subconsciously. Recognizing their own power to do harm engenders humility in Seers, destroying the folly of self-aggrandizement and the temptation to lord it over others.

Paradoxically, as some sage or crone said, "Sinners think they are saints; saints know they are sinners." Holiness, then, consists not in striving for perfection but in admitting that we are not perfect and in recognizing the depth of our sin. Thérèse of Lisieux, the Little Flower, developed this paradox well in her *spirituality of imperfection:* the more we admit we are empty and powerless, the more God can fill and empower us.

Heroic Seers are inherently humble. They know that, like everything else, they are interdependent. Their being depends on that of others. Thus, they form fellowships, as Gandalf did in *Lord of the Rings.* It was through the Fellowship of the Ring that evil was overcome, not by one magician acting on his own. The fellowship keeps Seers tied to human reality, keeps them compassionate, and makes their often solitary way less burdensome and lonely.

The great Seers know that, in the vast expanse of the cosmos, they are nothing without the Great Spirit, the Source of all power. Knowing that their Source forgives and redeems them and guided by their fellowship and their own insight, they are powerful yet humble, and divine grace and forgiveness radiate from them to others.

Understanding that spiritual power is the greatest power of all, and therefore the most susceptible to the lure of grandiosity, Seers befriend not only death, their Shadow, and their fellowship of like-minded souls, but also the *Trickster*. The inner Trickster is a minor archetype compared to the Sovereign, Warrior, Seer, and Lover, and indeed could be a subset of the Seer. In any case, it has a definite role to play, that is, pricking the bubble of self-aggrandizement.

In days gone by, healthy kings and queens had court jesters to prevent them from taking themselves too seriously. True Seers likewise either befriend an external Trickster or at least develop their own sense of humor. The Trickster, whether inner or outer, helps Seers laugh at their own foibles, makes them cognizant of the absurd and the downright silly, alleviates the pressure of solemn or sacred rituals or ceremonies, and combats dogmatism, perfectionism, prejudice, and self-righteousness.[21]

Tricksters keep all of us in touch with our own humanity and fallibility so we don't fall victim to our own folly. Comedians, satirists, and humorists who like to poke fun at religious leaders, while despised by some, actually do those religious leaders a great service.

To sum up, heroic Seers have been trained in secret knowledge and wisdom that they use in the service of others. The

Seer is a healer and miracle worker, not for show, but for the common good. The Seer is right-brained, that is, intuitive and holistic, and may have paranormal psychic powers. The Seer is the archetype of thoughtfulness, reflection, awareness, and insight. Seers integrate the opposites: masculine and feminine, rational and intuitive, darkness and light. By integrating their own Shadow, Seers harness their power in a constructive way. Since Seers align themselves with the cosmos and with God's will, they have great spiritual power. They guide rituals and initiation processes and channel energy and divine grace in a way that profoundly transforms people's lives.

THE HEROIC LOVER

The goal of the heroic Lover is bliss, oneness, unity with the beloved. The Lovers' fear is loss of love and disconnection. The Lovers' response to a dragon/problem is to love it. The Lovers' task is to follow their bliss and commit themselves to what they love. Their gift is commitment, passion, and ecstasy.[22]

Lovers love in four ways: *eros, philia, amor,* and *agape.* Eros involves the body, the feelings, and projection. We take all our longings and project them onto another person who we imagine can fulfill all our emotional and sexual needs. Falling in love means being seized or possessed by the Lover archetype. Philia is about bonding, whether between parent and child, siblings, friends, coworkers, or with some group such as a service club, mosque, synagogue, or church. Amor unites eros and philia, sexual love and friendship, in one union, usually within a marriage between a man and a woman.

Agape is sacrificial love. It is pure and unselfish and never thinks of compensation or reward. It is totally other-centered. Agape expresses itself in compassion and works of mercy toward the marginalized. It is the love Jesus spoke of in Matthew 25: feeding the hungry, clothing the naked, welcoming the stranger, visiting the sick and imprisoned. The Lover in agape wants to house the homeless and the geriatric psychiatric patient, to work in the slums of Calcutta, to die for the higher cause of serving humanity. It is found in every truly heroic Sovereign, Warrior, and Seer.

Normally, these four loves are not neatly separated. "The Lover archetype instead typically presents a tangled experience of generosity, neediness, sexual desire, affection, selfishness and passion all rolled into one. It has always been so."[23] However, all four of these loves have their source in the uniting, connecting, divine love that underlies all things. This primal energy expresses itself in our desires for food, sex, health, and meaning and in our drive to be fully alive and passionate in all our relations: to Mother Earth, our work, our families, our God.

Lovers feel at home with their body, with all sensual pleasures, and with sexuality, without unhealthy shame. They know they are a unity of body and soul, and so they see the body and its natural urges as positive and good, not as enemies. The Lover revels in life, in the joy of being embodied in the splendorful world of nature and in the joy of play, whether as sports, sex, humor, leisure, recreational reading, or imagination. Lovers connect more deeply with biological processes and unconscious urges and feelings than with the conscious ego, rationality, and logic. They live through their senses and so are enraptured by beautiful music, poetry, or art. Lovers experience all of life as art. They bring a sense of aesthetics to all they do.

Lovers sense the oneness of all things and feel at one with God. Since they are empathetically united to everything and everyone, they feel the pain of greedy exploitation of the Earth and its creatures. Their extreme sensitivity means they feel the suffering of others, of people being bombed in Iraq or carved up by machetes in African tribal warfare or overwhelmed by tsunamis. As St. Paul said, the true Lover bears all things and endures all things. Jesus was a man of sorrows and well-acquainted with grief. The more we love, the more we feel hurt for ourselves and for others. True love brings joy and pain, but the Lover embraces suffering, since suffering gives life its depth and profundity.

The Lover archetype calls us to innocence, to once again believe in the goodness of one's self, other people, and life. The hardened, cynical, sarcastic heart is foreign to the Lover. A refusal to close down and be numb, to shut life out with all its complications and harshness, means that the Lover is open to grief and mourning when life or love is lost.

Lovers see God as an exotic sensuous Being who enjoys good lovemaking — the *Shekina,* or *glory of God,* that hovers over the marriage bed in Kabbalistic thought. In Christian thought, because of the doctrine of the incarnation, we often say that God's only face, hands, arms, legs, and body in the world are our face, hands, arms, legs, and body. Therefore, it is not too much of a stretch to say that, from a Christian point of view, God does not just hover over the marriage bed; God gets right into the marriage bed with us and makes love to us through our marriage partner.

All of spirituality is rooted in the energy of the Lover archetype. Mystics seek the great orgasm, total oneness with the Great Lover. Mystics unite the Seer and the Lover. If mystics are married, they know that God comes to them most intensely through their partner. Through their partner, God can kiss and hug and hold and make love to them in a hands-on way, and they can love God back in the same way.

Healthy Lovers know that God blesses committed sexual relationships, that sex is holy, and that sex is a way to God. They neither unleash their sexual desires on everyone, becoming promiscuous, nor totally repress their sexual desires, becoming withered. Rather they channel all their sexual energy into one other person in a lifelong relationship. True Lovers are monogamous and sexually mature. They see the inner beauty of the opposite sex and relate to the whole person, not just to physical appearance. They are compassionate and sensitive on sexual matters. Since they have confronted and befriended their sexual Shadow, so that they control it rather than their Shadow controlling them, they approach sexuality with understanding, freedom, and celebration.

Lovers see that having a body is an essential part of being human. The body is not a prison for the soul or something evil. Lovers are not dualists. Matter is as holy as spirit in their eyes. They see that the body has been rejected, denied, and marginalized, and so they claim it, rejoice in it, and integrate it as a key element in their thinking about life. They study and wonder at all the marvels of the body, and treat it like it is — a sacred temple that the Spirit dwells in.

The Lover rejects overly moralistic, ascetic, and rationalistic religion, knowing that all these approaches can squeeze the vitality and love out of their adherents. Sometimes Jewish, Christian, and Muslim men have unconsciously projected their own Lover Shadow onto women, persecuting them as temptresses or seductresses, that is, as antiheroic modes of the female Lover. Since these men reject sensuality *in here*, they have to find a sexual object to reject *out there*. Their external world mirrors their inner reality.

True Lovers, whether male or female, rail against this type of injustice and any artificial, socially created conventions or laws that destroy love between people. At the same time Lovers know that morality, social conventions, and law and order have a place, and so they hold to a working tension between these and love, sensuality, and passion. Lovers' lives may be creative and unconventional, but they are not irresponsible. They know that both pleasure and boundaries for conduct, such as the Ten Commandments, are gifts from God.

Lovers know that the tension of opposites breeds creative energy. Just as the other heroic archetypes need the Lover, so the Lover needs the order, boundaries, and reflectiveness of the Sovereign, Warrior, and Seer. Lovers need the Sovereign to organize their feelings and sensuality, which otherwise would be chaotic rather than creative. They need the Warrior to cut through the sticky web of their attachments, so they can take decisive actions rather than be immobilized by trying to please everyone.

Lovers also need to activate their Warrior so they do not become doormats that everyone can use at their convenience. The Warrior can help with tough love, and the Seer can help with wide love. Lovers can be so passionate about their own family, nation, or religion that they exclude all others from their range of vision. The Seer can help the Lover to include everyone.

The Lover archetype is often opposed to the ego, which likes to have everything under control and ordered according to its own will. The Lover archetype may shatter the ego's safe world. If our soul feels *called* to something, it may not be able to resist the calling, in spite of all the ego's protestations. The divine may call the ego to let go of control, prudence, and practicality, fall in love, pursue the soul's bliss, try daring ventures, even go against our best judgment.

We might feel called to do things that seem irrational or absurd, as when Abraham felt called by God to sacrifice his son

Isaac after God had earlier promised that through Isaac all nations would be blessed. Isaac was spared after Abraham proved his unconditional faithfulness, and Abraham's willingness to trust God, not his own rationality, made him the father of three great religions.

Heroic Lovers use eros to fuel agape. They let their deep feelings motivate them to serve the poor. Rather than repressing eros, they let their *passion* become *compassion* and self-sacrifice in the name of justice. Just as Lovers respect their own body and the bodies of others, so they respect the body of their mother, the Earth. Their morals, ethics, and justice, as in Buddhism, extend to all sentient beings, not just humans. Eros makes them passionate about the sufferings of our planet and the myriads of creatures that depend on it. Their ecological awareness causes them to fight for the survival of all species.

True Lovers know how their soul works. They know that what they hate or admire in others is just a projection of their own dark or golden Shadows. Therefore, they readily forgive those they feel inclined to judge and learn from this what they judge within themselves, the parts of their soul they do not accept. They try to totally forgive and accept themselves and others and thus disempower their negative Shadow. Likewise, they are wary of worshiping others, since this is just their positive Shadow projecting their own hidden psychic treasures onto people out there.

Lovers try to own their whole soul, both the golden things and the dark things they try to hide, deny, and repress about themselves. Denying the positive and negative Shadow is simply the ego's way of resisting change and staying in control. Whenever we are forced to admit either our darkness or our greatness, forces outside of the ego are calling it to surrender to change. These forces are our true self and God. Our true self is striving to become whole by causing us to integrate our conscious ego and our unconscious Shadow. Only total self-acceptance can achieve this.

Lovers are about *being* and *feeling* more than *doing.* They are grounded in the rich sensory world of the here and now, smelling both the coffee and the roses. Love fills the world with vivid life and meaning and fills the Lover with energy and spirit. Lovers are idealists and dreamers of better worlds. They see to it that the Sovereign, Warrior, and Seer remain connected to the real world of suffering humanity. Without the Lover, the Sovereign, Warrior, and Seer could dwell in their castle, fortress, or ivory tower in comfortable detachment from life. The other archetypes need the Lover to help them fulfill their ultimate purpose — to take care of the human race.[24]

Lovers secure themselves in God's love because the only way we human beings can risk fully loving another person is through knowing that there is a never-ending love to fall back on if that person rejects us. Knowing that God's unconditional love undergirds their love, couples can freely disclose their deepest thoughts, vulnerabilities, and secrets to each other. God's love allows couples to be soul-mates.

For children to break out of their natural narcissism, they normally have to be loved intensely by their parents. Once they have received enough love, they are ready to give it. However, many people never felt totally loved by their parents, and therefore never became mature Lovers. They feel uncomfortable either being loved, because they do not believe they deserve it, or they feel unsure about giving love, since it may not be returned. Whether they live in rejection of others' attempts to love them or in narcissism, their existence will be sterile and isolated. For the Lover archetype to be activated fully, love must flow to and fro.

Men in particular have difficulty with being the beloved, with accepting love. Partly, this is because the beloved is less in control than the one giving the love. It is harder to receive than to give. The giver is considered superior to the receiver. Moreover, men have been taught by society and their parents to suppress their feminine side. They learn from an early age to hide and reject their softer, receptive side. This is what produces the *macho man* and his foolish male bravado that denies any weakness.

All four archetypes can easily become warped into antiheroic modes, which we will deal with next.

Summing up, heroic Lovers are committed to what they love. Lovers are passionate, ecstatic, generous, forgiving, romantic, sensual, and sexual in an ethical way. The Lover archetype is the archetype of life, connectedness, energy, and aliveness. It is about enjoyment and play, engagement with life, and seeking the oneness of all things. Lovers are full of gratitude and enthusiasm for everything. They are charismatic, creative, and artistic, and they follow their bliss. At the same time, they are grounded in the here and now. They integrate the body and the senses into their psyche. Since their senses are so alive, they are sensitive and vulnerable to the suffering of others and of the Earth. They embrace this pain and accept it as part of living a complete life. The Lover knows how to be loved as well as how to love. Like the other archetypes, Lovers need the balancing of the other three archetypes in order not to get trapped in their Shadow or antiheroic modes.

Chapter Five

THE ANTIHEROIC SOVEREIGN, WARRIOR, SEER, AND LOVER

THE NATURE OF THE SHADOW

The *Shadow* is what we hide, deny, or repress about ourselves, whether positive or negative. We can have great talent in a certain area, which others readily see, but to which we turn a blind eye or do not want to admit, because admitting it would logically imply a responsibility to use the talent, and using the talent could result in great and unpredictable life changes. It seems safer to just deny that the talent is there. The positive Shadow refers to the good in us that we repress but that often expresses itself within us in the people we admire and would secretly like to emulate.

Although there can be a positive side to the Shadow, for the purposes of this book, as already stated, we will focus on the negative side. Thus, when *Shadow* is referred to in the rest of this work, it signifies the *negative Shadow*.

The Shadow then refers to the dark, feared, unwanted side of the human personality, the side of a person's total potential that is repressed into the unconscious by the ego. The ego is the part of our psyche that determines what is allowed into consciousness and what is rejected. We each have a positive image of the type of person we want to be. For example, we may want to be seen as hardworking, and so we keep ourselves constantly busy. Since we are so hardworking, we may also have a secret desire to just relax and enjoy life. However, if we reject this desire and label it *sloth*, we will repress it into our unconscious, and it will form part of our Shadow. Through repeated lack of attention, this repressed desire can turn from a desire for leisure into a desire to actually be slothful. In the unconscious, it gathers energy until it begins to erupt arbitrarily into our conscious lives. We find ourselves being slothful when we really need to be diligent.

The Shadow is our personal storehouse of primitive, unconscious desires that conflict with accepted social norms. It expresses itself surreptitiously in our behavior as anger, lust, avarice, or any of the other seven deadly sins besides sloth. We may find that, in spite of who we would like to think we are, we sometimes act in crude, antisocial ways. It is not uncommon in spiritual direction to listen to directees express shock at their own behavior. They see themselves as nice, friendly, upbeat, and virtuous, and yet find themselves being petty, jealous, bitter, rude, or raging at their loved ones.

Like the shadow cast behind us by the sun, the Shadow travels with us, but we normally don't notice it. The Shadow is split-off, animal, instinctual energy. This energy, this animal side of who we are, is there as the result of millions of years of evolution.

The solution to the arbitrary expression of the Shadow in our behavior consists in raising Shadow tendencies to consciousness, being aware of them and allowing them to have a positive outlet. The more the Shadow is made conscious and integrated with the ego, the less power the Shadow has and the more strength and vigor the ego has. When Shadow and ego work in harmony, the person is full of energy, as the ego channels rather than obstructs the instincts.

Suppressing our animal side may allow us to function as part of a civilized society, but we also may lose a lot. Our emotions may become flattened and dull. Without spontaneity and creativity, we become boring and lack motivation to dream and achieve.

Repressed inner tendencies are primitive, unadapted, and awkward urges, but these urges are not evil in and of themselves. Good and evil lie in outward behavior, not in interior tendencies. The Shadow is not easily repressed; it is very tenacious. The same desire may keep coming up no matter how hard we try to suppress it. The Shadow strikes back eventually if not properly channeled. The more the animal side of us is repressed, the more it wants to rise like a destructive beast within us.

For example, a farmer may be a man of deep feeling. He may keep pushing down a desire to express his profound feelings in a poetic way, that is, he may repress his desire to write poetry. Rather than integrating this powerful urge to feel into his life by taking the time to write a little bit each day, he keeps suppressing his feelings. As he puts more and more energy into keeping the feelings down, the feelings become stronger and stronger until they overwhelm him, and he leaves his family and the farm and moves to the city to become a poet. He has thus thrown out everything he worked so long and hard to build, leaving a trail of devastated and dumbfounded people behind him.

This phenomenon is often called the *midlife crisis* or being seized by the *midlife crazies.* In our twenties and thirties, we had to suppress or ignore some parts of our personality that were not socially acceptable in order to survive in the adult world of work. These suppressed and ignored parts of ourselves get tossed into our "Shadow bag." At midlife we have less energy to keep the bag closed, and our Shadow urges start to emerge into consciousness. We can hold a beach ball under water only for so long, and we can keep our Shadow down only for so long. Eventually, it has to surface.

This can be frightening, but we have three basic options. We can exert even more energy in holding our repressed desires down and end up with ulcers, high blood pressure, or a heart attack. Alternatively, we can let all our unconscious stuff come up all at once and overwhelm us so that we do crazy things. Obviously, neither of these responses is healthy. Third, we can be aware that this unconscious material is coming up and demanding our attention, and we can decide what to do with it, and how to integrate it slowly into our lives so that we control it rather than it controlling us.

The Shadow can be like a child trying to get its mother's attention. At first the child tries positive things that will get noticed. If that fails, the child may become whiny and petulant. Failing still to get attention, it may become destructive. If still disregarded, the child goes through a kind of psychic death, shutting down its feelings and energy or becoming constantly restless for no apparent reason.

So it is with the Shadow. If we feel endlessly lethargic, think destructive thoughts, or feel uneasy, it may be that we are repeatedly ignoring some part of ourselves that is crying to be noticed. If we consciously allow this deep inner voice to speak to our heart and let it slowly turn up its volume, new life may flow through us as we discover our true voice and whole self.

Another danger with the Shadow is that it tends to get projected onto others. What we do not accept in ourselves we repress into our unconscious, and then we reject the same thing in others as well. Thus, the other person is always to blame, or is hated, as long as we are not aware of the darkness in ourselves.

The speck in the other person's eye is always more obvious to us than the log in our own.

Exposure of the Shadow in analysis usually encounters great resistance. People are afraid that their ego, which they have painstakingly constructed by rejecting all this darkness, will collapse if the Shadow is let into consciousness. It takes a great deal of maturity to accept your Shadow, withdraw all your projections, stop blaming and hating others, and know that you are the source of your own problems.[1]

The Shadow is particularly powerful when the archetypes are involved. According to Jung, when the archetypal images are not made conscious, they are most dangerous. Without being aware of it, a person may succumb to the overwhelming power of an archetype and become *possessed* by it.[2] As stated earlier, each of the four heroic archetypes has two Shadow forms or poles. One pole represents total possession, and the other pole represents total nonpossession by the heroic form of the archetype. Thus, as we shall now see, the Sovereign becomes a Tyrant or Abdicator, the Warrior becomes a Sadist or Masochist, the Seer becomes a Manipulator or a Fool, the Lover becomes an Addict or Frigid. Health, and therefore freedom, in relation to an archetype is to be neither possessed nor dispossessed by it, but rather to have a healthy balance of attachment to it and detachment from it, and thus to express it in its positive, heroic form.

The following archetypes may seem lower-than-life, and it may be hard to believe that anyone that bad could exist. This is because, once again, the archetypes are being presented in their pure form, this time in their Shadow mode. However, in day-to-day life, real human beings are a mixture of the good and the bad. Presenting them in their purely negative form here makes it easier for us to clearly understand what the antiheroic archetypes are like. Again, the descriptions below are an attempt to integrate the work of Moore and Gillette, Bly, Pearson, and others.

THE TYRANT AND ABDICATOR

Antiheroic Sovereigns abound. We all have directly experienced, or at least heard of, Tyrants. Sometimes the Tyrant is an overbearing parent, a rageaholic boss or superior, or a corrupt politician. Hitler, Stalin, and Mao are classic twentieth-century examples, and the Bible is full of ancient ones, for example, King Herod, King Saul, and Pharaoh.

Once Tyrants identify their ego with the Sovereign archetype, they first become possessed by it and then become paranoid they will lose their power. So Herod's paranoia about the coming king, the Messiah, leads him to have all the male babies in Bethlehem put to death, and similarly Saul's paranoia results in his repeated attempts to kill God's anointed servant, David.

Pharaoh is another classic antiheroic Sovereign. He fully oppresses and exploits his Hebrew slaves, and when they become too numerous and powerful, he, like Herod, orders the death of their male babies. Oppressors always seek to destroy the Warrior energy of the oppressed, to break their spirit, to put their masculine side to death, to make them believe they are helpless victims. Fortunately for all of us, God heard the cries of the poor Hebrews and sent to them a heroic Warrior-Seer named Moses, who was willing to do whatever his Sovereign-God demanded.[3]

Biblical Tyrants are not just male. Queen Jezebel arranged to have a law abiding citizen, Naboth, unjustly framed and killed so that her husband, King Ahab, could have Naboth's fine vineyard. Slaughter of innocent people is common with Tyrants. Queen Herodias told her daughter Salome to ask for John the

Baptist's head on a platter because he protested against her incestuous marriage.

Tyrants love their power and believe that if they lose it they are nothing. This leads to suspicion of any other shining stars in the firmament. They see any subordinate who is successful, talented, or popular with the people as a potential threat. Tyrants lack inner authority, integrity, and security. To quell their fears they become overcontrolling and oppressive, which their subjects eventually rebel against. This rebellion generates further paranoia in the Tyrant, and more oppression, in an ever escalating spiral, until the Tyrant slaughters great numbers or is deposed.

Saddam Hussein regularly invited his generals to dine with him and then after the meal executed any who disagreed with him on any issue or who he suspected might try to overthrow him. He even did this with relatives!

As parents or spouses, Tyrants are tyrannical. They want total control over their partner or children or both. They have great difficulty with allowing their spouse or children to grow up and claim their own manhood or womanhood. Tyrants paradoxically have low self-esteem, and this causes them to feel threatened by any growth in knowledge or strength in their children. They may assault their own progeny verbally, physically, or even sexually. Their children's hopes and dreams are disparaged and their successes ignored. Any exuberance or joy is summarily put down. Often they drive their spouses and children out of the home. They see their partner as inferior rather than equal and want to block their education and career so their partner can remain the Tyrant's personal servant.

Tyrants are narcissists. They imagine themselves enthroned at the center of a universe of their own making, surrounded by subjects whose only purpose in life is to serve them. In some cases, they even seek to be worshiped as a god, as a way of being reassured of their sovereignty.

In the business world, they show up as male or female corporate executives whose only interest is their career trajectory: they are not concerned with being good and just stewards of their realm, that is, the company and its people. Their devotion is not to the company but to themselves and their own financial benefit. They don't care how many employees they fire, as long as they make more and more profit.

Inside every Tyrant lurks the opposite dimension, the inner Abdicator, who makes up for a lack of genuine power by overcompensation: inner Abdicators overidentify with the Sovereign archetype and become Tyrants. Tyrants hate criticism because it exposes their hidden weakness. Their inner Abdicator, who feels they are nothing in and of themselves, tries to hide their weakness in their Shadow, and then projects their hatred of their own weakness onto others, attacking and destroying anyone who appears weak in any way. Tyrants may react to criticism with rage, but this is just a guise for their feelings of worthlessness and impotence.

For the Tyrant, their ego is God. By identifying with the Sovereign archetype rather than using it to serve others, the way God intended it to be used, the Tyrant's inflated ego usurps the throne of the One True Sovereign, that is, God. Satan, in Christian mythology, was the first to attempt this palace coup and, with the other rebel angels, has been trying ever since to persuade human beings to follow suit.

The mythological serpent in the Garden of Eden knew that the ultimate temptation was to be like God. Today the forbidden fruit is money, the Great Idol we sacrifice everything to, because it gives us the illusion that we no longer are dependent upon God, belong to God, and need God, for we *are* God, and we can do anything we want and have total control over our lives, as long as we have enough money. However, as Jesus said, money does not make our lives secure. Our arrogance thus cuts us off from divine wisdom, the wisdom that knows that life is fleeting.

Tyrants totally identify with the Sovereign archetype because that is the only way their inner Abdicator feels it can get self-worth and power. However, the inner Abdicator may also choose to totally disidentify with the archetype, so that the true Abdicator visibly emerges. Although we all have latent Sovereign energy within us, the Abdicators' access to this is so blocked that they feel completely impotent. Abdicators often project the Sovereign energy so deeply buried in their Shadow onto someone else and become dependent on the other to make them feel secure.

We all know of families where the members are codependent, or one spouse has no identity apart from the other, or single parents either have no life without their children or totally dominate them. And most of us have experienced work situations where everything revolves around the whims of the boss, or some bullying coworker, and everyone tiptoes around that person.[4] Abdicators and Tyrants tend to cocreate each other and go hand-in-hand.

In the Roman Catholic Church (which I simultaneously love and feel free to constructively criticize, since it is my own tradition) many laypeople are Abdicators. Laity often ascribe to priests and bishops far more power than they actually have, and some clergy pick up on this and start to believe they have unlimited authority and can do whatever they want with impunity.

Since there are so few priests, bishops are desperate to hold on to them, and thus give them too much autonomy and power.

Some priests become like little kings or gods in their own par-ish. Since priests are in the dual role of spiritual Sovereign and spiritual Seer in their realm, they have double the archetypal power, with no one really there to keep them in check. No won-der Tyrants emerge. Combine this with priests who feel called to the priesthood but not called to celibacy, and no wonder sexual abuse happens!

Perhaps all this would be remedied by allowing priests to marry, so that more men would seek the priesthood and bishops would have more priests to choose from. Bishops could then exert more healthy control. If a priest misbehaved, he could be more easily dismissed. Eliminating mandatory celibacy for priests might be one of the best things the church could do in attracting men back into its fold. It might solve one of the basic problems of power in the Roman Catholic Church, that is, the problem of both priestly and lay Tyrants and Abdicators.

In any human organization, whether churches, families, businesses, or governments, the *abdication of power* syndrome of the Abdicator can be just as disastrous as the *usurpation of power* syndrome of the Tyrant. Abdicators hate and fear respon-sibility, being a leader, and being in authority. They let things get out of control.

The Abdicator is the man or woman who would *not* be king or queen. Abdicators are too wrapped up in narcissism to generate new life in anyone. They slough off the heavy cloak of maturity, adulthood, and just government. All decisions are made by con-sulting the polls, by asking others to decide for them. They are nice, gentle, sensitive, accommodating, and totally ineffectual, letting their realm gradually run itself into the ground.

Tyrants say whatever serves them. As Abdicators, false priests, bishops, ministers, prophets, and leaders of any kind just say whatever people want to hear rather than the truth. Thus, both

Tyrant and Abdicator speak untruth. They warp the truth to fit whatever meets their own needs, whether to be in control or out of control. Neither Tyrant nor Abdicator truly listens to or serves God or people.

Tyrants think nothing of exploiting and abusing others. They ruthlessly and mercilessly pursue their own self-interests, never feeling the pain of others. Tyrants get others to do their will by manipulation, intimidation, and force. Saddam Hussein's sons had Iraqi Olympic athletes tortured if they did not win a medal.

All those who live under a Tyrant have to sacrifice their dreams and desires to the whims and moods of the Tyrant. No one is allowed to feel anything, because only the Tyrant's feelings count.

And Tyrants have only two basic feelings: fear and rage. Their constant fear results in an insatiable desire for absolute control. If they cannot force someone to kowtow to their way, they throw a tantrum and punish everyone. Like the Red Queen in *Alice in Wonderland*, they yell "off with their heads" at the slightest provocation. Some bosses adopt the attitude that "the floggings will continue until morale improves"!

Besides fear and rage, the only other emotion of Tyrants is transitory delight whenever their inordinate lust for status, power, and personal aggrandizement is fulfilled. Tyrants are "selfish, narrowminded . . . and prone to either indolence and self-indulgence or spartan rigidity and intolerance."[5]

Tyrants love to be their own law and accountable to no one. They believe they are accountable neither to God nor other humans, except perhaps those who support them in some way, either financially or through votes. They try to be totally free of others' control if possible. Having brutally severed any ties with God, others, and their own humanness, they have no interest in serving the poor, or in justice. Their scarcity mentality sees others' losses as their gain and others' gain as their loss.

Young people feel cursed rather than blessed if their only role models are Tyrants or Abdicators. If their leaders are either dictators or impotent, they cannot develop their own inner Sovereign in a healthy way, or their own natural idealism. The young want and need mentors who are honorable, honest, and responsible. They cannot follow those they have no respect for. Antiheroic Sovereigns who live disordered and corrupt lives are not attractive to young people.

Both Tyrant and Abdicator misuse their power. Whether using too much power or too little, they harm others either by intention or neglect. They both need to learn to use power to create abundance for all, rather than pleasure for themselves. If they surrender to the temptation to be self-centered, they will end up feeling empty and sterile. Worse yet, they will make everyone feel cynical and fearful and drag everyone down with them. Antiheroic Sovereigns live their fears, that is, they live in an isolated hell rather than fulfilling their dreams, and those of their people, and living with them in heaven.[6]

In summary, the antiheroic Sovereign as Tyrant is fearful, uncentered, paranoid, and destructive. Tyrants are suspicious, jealous, insecure, and death-dealing. They see new life, creativity, and strength in others as a threat. They have no sense of inner order, peace, authority, and integrity. Their own disordered desires cause them to constantly seek power, status, and self-aggrandizement. They need constant reassurance that they are in control. The Tyrant is arrogant, authoritarian, and wants to be adored, or even worshiped as a god. Their ego, not God, is sitting on the throne of their life. Their fear of losing control of the realm causes them to be ruthless, merciless, abusive, and unjust in every way. They exploit others for their own gain and believe others exist only to serve them. Their overidentification with the Sovereign archetype causes them to believe they *are* the Sovereign archetype rather than its *servant*, as God intended them to be.

The antiheroic Sovereign as Abdicator shows up in two ways. In one way, Abdicators are behind every Tyrant. They overcompensate for their sense of powerlessness by overidentifying with the Sovereign archetype. They mask their weakness with rage, insisting on their way and humiliating those who are weak. They hate their own weakness, project it onto others, and then hate and attack them. They are defensive, hostile, cruel, and tormented by fears of disloyalty. They need power over others to feel any sense of self-worth.

On the other hand, Abdicators may totally disidentify with the Sovereign archetype and see themselves as completely powerless and incapable of decisive action, or of feeling calm and in authority. They may be overly nice, sensitive, and gentle, but they refuse to lead, take responsibility, or generate life in others. They tend to be dependent on someone else for power, or codependent in relating to others. By letting things get out of healthy control, they are just as destructive as the Tyrant.

THE SADIST AND MASOCHIST

Every major religion considers detachment from this world to be an honorable virtue. For the Warrior, detachment allows cool and calm assessment of any situation. However, if not balanced with the other archetypes, the Warrior can become too detached, Warrior energy turns cruel, and the Sadist emerges from the Shadow. Terrorists everywhere detach themselves totally from compassion. With the Lover completely out of the way, they can crash planes into the World Trade Center, explode car bombs, or machine gun an ambulance or a school bus without any thought of the innocent victims involved.

Sadists can be cruel with or without feeling. In the latter case, the Sadist is the soldier "just doing my job" of systematically killing and torturing people, or "just following orders from on high," as many of Hitler's SS troops claimed when interrogated about their sins against the Jews. In the former case, the Sadists with feelings, extreme fear leads to extreme anger and a frenzy of destruction, as in witch hunts in Salem, or lynchings of blacks by the Ku Klux Klan.

Often Sadists feel their self-concept as the pure race or superior tribe or religion is threatened. Al Qaeda Muslims act out of fear that secular Western values will corrupt Islam. False Warriors are always conveniently blind to their own unethical tactics. True Warriors are aware of their Shadow and therefore have a sense of humility.

Rather than trying to understand their opponent, Shadow Warriors objectify their opponent as the *enemy*, and thus can make the enemy purely evil and inhuman, as the U.S. propaganda machine did with the Soviet Union and the Taliban. This then justifies nonnegotiation, the antiheroic Warrior using any means to defeat the enemy, and killing with no sense of remorse for the loss of human life. The Sadist in fact loves carnage. General George Patton, surveying a battlefield strewn with dead bodies and burned out tanks, reportedly yelled out, "God, how I love this!"

If a nation believes that it is purely good and an enemy nation is a purely evil empire, anything can be rationalized, even dropping atomic bombs on civilians, as happened at Hiroshima and Nagasaki. Two hundred thousand innocent people instantly burned alive is conveniently overlooked as long as a nation believes in its own innocence and refuses to look at its own evil.

The Sadist's goal is to totally crush, mangle, and finally kill the enemy, not just defeat them. No prisoners are taken unless the Sadist intends to torture them. Often the Sadist, out of pure perversity, thinks of something more fiendish than merely killing the enemy: they rape the enemy's wives and daughters in front of them, or cut off the enemy's hands so they will be forever a burden to their own people. This was a favorite tactic of the Hutus in their campaign against the Tutsis.

In nonmilitary life, Sadists are still at war. They despise anyone weak or vulnerable and therefore abuse their children or beat their spouses. While it is wife-beating that usually gets into the news, some experts believe that beating of married men may happen more often than anyone has suspected, but men are much more reluctant to report it because it carries a tremendous load of shame for a man to admit being physically beaten by a woman.

We know from the war in Iraq, with pictures of female soldiers torturing and humiliating male prisoners of war in Abu Ghraib prison, that women are capable of being Sadists too. However, as I have written earlier, men need to change more than women. False male Warriors always promote patriarchy, in which immature men control everything, particularly the female body. Male Sadists teach women to repress their inner Warrior so that to get any protection a woman has to give her body to a man.

Antiheroic Warriors, whether male or female, battle against the power of the feminine within them, and against everything soft and relational. Their fear of the feminine leads them to wanton brutality against both men and women. This is seen in the drill sergeant who feels he has to humiliate and violate the men in his charge, or in the workplace in female bosses who put down, harass, and unjustly fire employees. If no other archetypes are developed, Shadow Warriors are continually embattled and perceive everything as a slight, threat, or challenge to be confronted.

The Shadow Warrior is a villain who uses Warrior skills for personal gain without thought of morality or ethics. Typical of this is the archetypal dream had by a young man: "I am a soldier of fortune in ancient China. I have been creating a lot of trouble, hurting a lot of people, disturbing the order of the empire for my own profit and benefit. I'm a kind of outlaw, a kind of mercenary."[7]

Not just those in the military, but also revolutionaries and activists may be under the power of the Sadist, using violent means to achieve their goals. In the French Revolution, the revolutionaries simply beheaded their opponents with guillotines. Mahatma Gandhi warned his followers about forgetting about nonviolence and replacing one pack of wolves (the British) with another (themselves). It is easy for the oppressed to become what they hate — the Tyrants they seek to oust.

Negative Warriors have no humane feelings or higher values or ideals; they are just out for money, status, and power. The Sadist is rampant in the business world today in the form of hostile takeovers and chief executive officers ruthlessly downsizing people to make more profit. For Sadists there is always a craving to beat others, either literally, symbolically, or socially. They have to be better than others, to get ahead, which means to leave others behind, to win and be on top at all costs, to be superhuman, even if it means compromising every principle. It was the sadistic Nazis, based on Nietzsche, who wanted the pure race, which meant getting rid of anyone weak, in order to create the *übermensch*, the *overman*.

Negative Warriors divide the world into only two camps: those who block them and must be destroyed, and those who give in, and therefore are weak and must be subjugated. Sadists see things in black and white. You are either on their side or against them. They fight to preserve injustice, either consciously or unconsciously. For example, although they may be just doing their jobs, police defending so-called free trade meetings are fighting for the rights of transnational corporations instead of the common good. Likewise, protestors who become violent obstruct the cause of the true Warriors, the nonviolent demonstrators. Violent protestors become Gandhi's pack of wolves and inadvertently preserve injustice.

The Shadow Warrior can take many unhealthy forms. A common one in our competitive society is the workaholic, who actually becomes a Sadist toward himself or herself. Shadow Warriors in the form of the Sadist tend to become compulsive, competing so hard and so long that they don't know when to stop. Workaholics, in an attempt to alleviate the anxiety generated by low self-worth or job insecurity become overly rigorous, denying their pain and exhaustion, until they burn out.

Workaholics may feel that burnout happens because they are so committed to their cause, whether it is social workers fighting for the poor, therapists or doctors fighting to save their patients' lives, ministers or evangelists fighting to save souls, or businessmen fighting for their business. In reality, it may not be that workaholics possess a cause; it maybe that the Shadow Warrior archetype possesses them. Therefore, they are constantly embattled, constantly fighting whoever and whatever gets in their way. They deny their inner Lover, so they never just relax and enjoy life. And they deny their inner Seer, so they never admit that their opponent has a valid point of view as well.

The Sadist and Masochist, like the Tyrant and Abdicator, are inseparable. The Sadist, by overdoing everything, can inadvertently become a Masochist. Fueled by impossibly high standards, workaholics can mercilessly drive themselves and everyone around them night and day, until breakdown occurs. They can ignore the feelings, needs, and warning signs coming from others and from their own body. Suddenly, key employees quit, their spouse leaves, they have a stroke or coronary. Not knowing their own and others' limits, they never know when to quit, until their life becomes self-punishing.

Masochists feel they lack both boundaries and defenses. Whereas Sadists focus exclusively on getting their own way, Masochists let others have their way at the Masochist's expense. They project onto others the Warrior energy they have buried so deeply within themselves, so that others are experienced as omnipotent. Masochists, feeling they have no bastions to guard their body, mind, or soul, allow others to push them around and verbally or physically abuse them. Masochists let other people violate the limits of the Masochists' self-respect and psychic health. They are longsuffering victims.

If Masochists take too much abuse for too long, they may eventually explode into verbal or even physical violence. The Sadist lies just below the Masochist's passivity, just as the Masochist underlies the Sadist's rage. This explains how a formerly docile employee can return after being fired and gun down his boss, or how a passive wife can suddenly cut off her husband's genitals.

Masochists dominated by others live in a prison. They have no balancing focus in their lives and no self-respect, since their lives are dictated to them by others. Masochists don't know how to say no, be assertive, and stand up for themselves. Typically, they have neglected their own needs and desires for so long that they don't even know what their desires are anymore. Without an inner Warrior, Masochists lack vigor, resolve, and courage. They flee like cowards from confrontation. They may dream, but their dreams remain ephemeral wisps. Dreams never become reality because Masochists cannot endure the pain necessary to accomplish them and believe they will fail before they even begin.

Marriage, the most intimate of human relationships, often brings forth the inner Sadist or Masochist. Some masochistic spouses endure years of abuse because their partner has destroyed their self-esteem to the point that they believe they could not survive on their own. Sadistic spouses love to inflict verbal damage that poisons their partner's soul. If there is physical violence, the attacker, whether male or female, has become possessed by Kali, the Hindu goddess of destruction, who wants blood and smashed skulls.

Kali is a religious expression of the Sadist archetype, as are legalistic and ascetic men in every religion who see themselves as spiritual Warriors justified in keeping the corrupting influence of women's bodies under wraps and veils, as the Taliban did. Nowadays, there are women, at least in some religious orders within Christianity, who similarly see men as the corrupting ones and so fight against everything male. They claim everything bad is caused by males, or patriarchy, and everything good comes from females.

The Christian church, or at least some church hierarchies, have proven in the past that they can become spiritual Sadists, for example, in the Crusades, where avenging Christian warriors killed people in the name of Jesus. In the Inquisition, good was identified with total subservience to church authority, and bad was identified with any kind of freethinking, which was labeled as rebellion, and which then justified the use of torture. The Mennonite *Martyr's Mirror* gives a detailed account of a time when the Roman Catholic Church allowed itself to be possessed by the Sadist archetype. In Latin America, the conquistadors gave the Aztecs and Incas a clear choice: be baptized or be strangled to death. In Germany, between 1550 and 1650, twenty-six thousand "witches" were put to death by Protestant churches. Fortunately, nowadays churches are far more enlightened.

Spiritual sadism is one extreme. On the other hand, as Robert Bly says, ministers and priests can be too accommodating, charming, and nice: "Contemporary ministers channel spiritual comfort, coddling and soothing, but at the expense of risk-taking and solitariness. Many a male minister gives up his longing for solitude" and replaces it with "a longing for comfort, for peace in the house, for padded swords, for protective coloration, a longing to be the quail hiding in fall reeds."[8]

In other words, male ministers and priests often repress bravery and openness to change. As spiritual Masochists, they put aside their own beliefs and what they would like to say about justice in order to be kind to their congregation. They then feel like they have lost their integrity and their soul. Until churches of every denomination replace Tyrants, Abdicators, Sadists, and Masochists with healthy Sovereigns and Warriors, not many men will be attracted to them.

To sum up, the antiheroic Warrior as Sadist can act cruelly with or without passion. When passionate, Sadists act violently out of anger or fear. Their objectification of the enemy as purely evil allows them to kill without any remorse and to even delight in the destruction or torture of others. They are continually embattled with those around them, and, whether they are male or female, continually battle with the feminine within themselves.

They have no compassion for the weak, no ethics or higher values or ideals. They compromise every principle in order to win. Winning, that is, furthering their own interests, is everything. They look out only for themselves.

Antiheroic Warriors as Masochists project Warrior energy onto others, do not defend themselves, and let others walk over them and run their lives. They have no boundaries, and so others can verbally, physically, or even sexually abuse them. However, if pushed by others too much, they may uncharacteristically explode. Normally, the Masochist is passive, avoids confrontation, and is too accommodating of others. The interests of others always come before the Masochist's interests. Masochists lack vigor and determination and are cowardly. They cannot endure pain or hardship and feel defeated before they even begin. They may feel they are never good enough and so mercilessly work themselves into an early grave. They ignore danger signs regarding their health and relationships until things fall apart. Masochists feel like they have lost their integrity and their soul.

THE MANIPULATOR AND FOOL

The wise man and wise woman are aware of the potential to misuse Seer power, and they guard against it. They know that the mantle of the Seer can be worn only with proper humility. One of the heroic Seers' main values is the compassionate application of their gifts.

However, the antiheroic Seer, in the form of the Manipulator, is not concerned with the proper use of spiritual power. Manipulators play on people's fears, misrepresent the facts, and distort the truth in order to deceive the innocent. They seek out the needy and vulnerable, those who are dependent or co-dependent, or who have difficulty saying no to someone in a position of authority. Manipulators violate trust and confidentiality and take advantage of others' weakness for their own gain, charging heavily for the information they give, which is usually just intended to impress people with their learning and superiority. When it comes to rituals of initiation, Manipulators do not guide people by degrees that they can handle and integrate into their lives; they insensitively flood them with information and techniques before they are ready for them. Like the Sadist, the Manipulator detaches from human suffering to the point of being cruel.

Manipulators show up in every profession. In medicine, Manipulators greedy for money help their patients become addicted to drugs or schedule unnecessary appointments or surgery. A cartoon showed a surgeon saying to a patient lying on the operating table, "Is this surgery necessary? Why, without it I won't be able to take my Bahamas vacation this year!"

In the legal profession, Manipulators word documents in unnecessarily complex legalese to keep clients dependent upon them for translation, exacerbate conflict between separating or divorcing spouses, or delay legal processes so they benefit from the interest on trust funds.

Therapists withhold information clients need to get better in order to keep them coming back. For example, a therapist might not tell a client about another therapist who specializes in treating the particular problem the client has.

Manipulating doctors, lawyers, and therapists all convey that they have great wisdom and hidden knowledge that the average person must pay a lot to access. They use their secret knowledge for their own purposes first, and only secondarily to benefit others. Manipulators also show up as politicians who hide their real agenda and tell the public whatever it wants to hear in order to be reelected. Or the Manipulator may be an advertising executive who subliminally manipulates the public, or a media professional who, by withholding certain information or by writing from a particular worldview, generates a public mindset favored by big business, which pays the person behind the scenes.

By being false with people, by being secretive, and by outright lying, Manipulators destroy themselves, as well as deceiving others. By severing authentic relatedness to other human beings, their cynicism isolates them from innocence, purity, sincerity, and goodness. By using their knowledge to humiliate, hurt, and control others, they become dangerous charlatans rather than sophisticated, as they imagine themselves to be.

In the academic world, Manipulators claim knowledge they do not really possess, and then, if found out, they attempt to cover their ignorance with a web of rhetoric that sounds learned but says nothing. They are clever but not wise. In spite of knowing a lot, they are foolish. Knowledge makes them arrogant. They delight in putting down students who question them, or they get so caught up in theories that they overlook people.

Manipulators cut themselves off not only from people but also from important functions of their own soul. In arguing with everyone in order to get their way, Manipulators become too rational and analytical and shut down their dreams, imagination, emotions, and intuition. Whether male or female, they close off the feminine side of the soul that is in touch with the unconscious, nonrational, and mysterious. They become coldhearted, dogmatic, and judgmental, detached voyeurs of life who live in their head rather than in the real world. Excessive devotion to their own theories of how the world *should* work may make it difficult to interact with the world *as it is*. Thinking too much results in ineffective engagement with life.

Evil is basically the diminishment of ourselves or others. Manipulators use, in a negative way, the Seer's power of re-visioning who someone is. Thus, the Manipulator labels a child "loony" or "silly" rather than "imaginative." They refer to someone by their illness or their problem. For example, they say that a boy is a juvenile delinquent, as if that encompasses all that he is. Rather than seeing Eileen Jones, who loves opera and is the devoted mother of three children, they dehuman-ize her as the Alzheimer problem on Ward Two. She is now a statistic so the Manipulator can get more funding. Manip-ulators diminish people by renaming and labeling them in a way that limits and stigmatizes them or by making negative predictions such as "you'll never amount to anything," which becomes, not surprisingly, a self-fulfilling prophecy.

The Manipulator is possessed by the Seer archetype and uses knowledge for power over others, whereas the Fool feels totally bereft of the Seer's wisdom. The Fool is more denying and pas-sive than the Manipulator, and therefore much more elusive and slippery. Whereas the Manipulator sabotages others fairly overtly, the Fool is much more covert. The Fool wants Seer power but not Seer responsibility. Fools are not interested in properly teaching or initiating others, or in properly contain-ing and channeling power for everyone's benefit. Fools operate out of envy and a desire to subtly destroy the achievements or progress of others.

Fools commit sins of both commission and omission, but feign an impenetrable wall of naiveté. If confronted about their hidden hostile motives, Fools will act bewildered, question our intuitions about them, and accuse us of paranoia. However, behind the smoke-screen of innocence we will still sense covert manipulation.

Fools want, at all costs, to avoid the pain of journeying into their own internal desolation. Sorting out their inner chaos is too difficult for them, so they remain on the surface and create the illusion of power for themselves by being passive-aggressive. Thus, Fools never get in touch with their feelings, undergo inner liberation, or learn from their mistakes. The only learning they want is how to block and derail others. The Fool is present whenever anyone runs from self-knowledge. Their claim to be innocent of any wrongdoing may be sincere, because they may have hidden their ill intentions so well that they are not even fully aware of their secret motives themselves.

Whereas true Seers can laugh at themselves or laugh *with* others, false Seers laugh *at* others. Humor, in the hands of the Manipulator or Fool, turns into sarcasm. Derision is the Fool's weapon of choice. Often Fools will deride others for things they are doing themselves. While the true Seer employs the Trickster to deflate any of the Seer's temptations to grandiosity, both the Manipulator and Fool deflate others in order to inflate their own delusions of grandeur.

Manipulators are foolish, and Fools are manipulative, so they both have Fools and Manipulators within, it is just that the Fool is even more subtle than the Manipulator. Tricksters play tricks to reveal the truth, but Fools play tricks to hide the truth so well that they half-believe their own proclaimed innocence.

Seeing is a powerful drug, so the true Seer must constantly fight the strong pull to become addicted. Seers possessed by the archetype can easily start to believe they *are* God rather than the *instrument* of God. This is the perennial temptation of anyone giving spiritual guidance or direction, whether as a Hindu

guru, Catholic priest, Muslim ayatollah, Protestant televange-
list, or New Age shaman. God will not tolerate such perverse
spiritual arrogance for long, so the false Seer inevitably comes
to ruin. Humility is the foremost virtue of Seers, lest they do
great harm.

In summary, antiheroic Seers as Manipulators are motivated
by lust for spiritual power, and thus they play on people's fears,
distort the truth, and use their power to harm, not heal. They
manipulate the needy, violate their trust, and lie to them, or
withhold vital information that could help them. They use
their knowledge to belittle and control others for their own
advantage, not to serve them. They are cynical and detached
from others and label people in a way that diminishes their
self-esteem. Denigrating intuition, imagination, dreams, and
feelings, they overemphasize reason and theories, live in their
head, and observe and manipulate life rather than living it. All
of this makes them cold and heartless.

Antiheroic Seers as Fools hide hostile motives behind feigned
naiveté. Their envy of those who live and have authentic,
healthy power causes them to be passive-aggressive and to
engage in covert destruction of others in a perverse and back-
handed way of gaining status. They use humor in the form of
sarcasm to put others down. They are essentially dishonest,
shirking and denying responsibility. They are slippery and elusive when confronted with wrongdoing. Although they have
no authentic power, they have grandiose imaginings about
themselves.

For both Manipulators and Fools, their ego-inflation causes
them to see themselves as the *Source* rather than the *instrument* of wisdom. Both the Fool and the Manipulator are out of
touch with the Deep Spirit of the cosmos.

The Addict and Frigid

The Shadows of the heroic Lover are the antiheroic Addict and the Frigid. The Addict's greatest problem is lack of limits, that is, boundaries. Addicts want unlimited sensual and sexual pleasure, and this is their undoing. Limits and boundaries give us a sense of place, differentiation, and identity. Without them we are lost. Addicts drown in a limitless ocean of sensory experience, sucked up in a tornado of sensuality over which they have no control. A classic example is Vincent Van Gogh, overwhelmed by swirling colors, which eventually drove him to insanity and suicide.

Addicts have to learn that structure is their best friend, not something constricting, and that discipline is their most prized possession, as scripture says. Often, it is only physical, marital, financial, or spiritual ruin that wakes Addicts up and causes them to draw up the limits of their life.

In relationships, Addicts are fickle and promiscuous. When things get tough, they move on. So although they may have many lovers, they have few friends. Since they are committed to no one, they project this onto others and believe that no one is committed to them.

Constantly trying to fill the hole in their soul, their aching loneliness, makes Addicts narcissistic. Focusing on taking rather than giving ensures the destruction of future relationships, which increases their sense of isolation and desperation. They are desperate for love. Giving in to temptation, they have sex without love, the titillation leaves them unsatisfied, and so they pursue further thrills they hope will fill them, in a never-ending merry-go-round of destruction.

Sex and relationship Addicts are consumed by jealousy, envy, infatuation, and obsession. They may get perverse satisfaction out of getting others addicted, luring others from productive lives or happy marriages, or experiencing the thrill of sexual conquest, as if it was a safari hunt and the opposite sex was their prey.

Monogamy derives from a person's choice to live a centered, calm, and stable life. However, people addicted to promiscuity or pornography are internally fragmented. Promiscuous persons leave a bit of their soul with each person they have sex with. Pornography Addicts focus on fragments of others' anatomy. They never see the sexual object as a whole person, a unity of body, soul, heart, and mind with emotions and dreams and memories and a whole life. Both promiscuity and pornography Addicts never treat others as complete human beings whom they could respect and with whom they could have a committed relationship.

Addicts are idolatrous in that they make fleeting, relative, and fragmentary experiences their Absolute. They are looking for a fix that will satisfy them once-and-for-all, but only God can do that. It is the limits of finite things — drugs, men, or women — that keeps them searching for the eternal high or orgasm.

Ultimately, Addicts are idolaters of the self, since their ego is attempting to do what only God can do, that is, love every fragment. What Addicts think they need is to be one with everything, like God. However, what they really need is a Oneness that stands outside themselves and issues commandments that put boundaries on their lives. "You shall come this far and no further, unless you want to be destroyed," says the Lord. This is the only Oneness that can bring calm and stability to the Addict.

Being caught up in *maya* or *samsara*, the illusory, intoxicating, ever shifting dance of forms and pleasures, results in

Addicts not being able to organize or be in control of themselves. The spider web of sensory enmeshment means that they cannot detach and gain distance and perspective on their lives. The essence of addiction is to not see the overall pattern: the incessant attempt to fill their emptiness with things other than God, things that do not satisfy but only make them hungrier, eternally restless and searching, unable to settle down and be content. Only when Addicts see the overall pattern of their lives and where it is taking them can they see the light and begin to reform.

Addicts lack boundaries between their conscious and unconscious minds, but it is out of the unbounded chaos of the unconscious that form and structure emerge. The archetypes structure the collective unconscious and give it the form and content that is needed. The Addict needs the heroes, the healthy archetypes, to create boundaries, because it is only through heroic effort that boundaries can be constructed for the Addict.

Addicts need the heroic Sovereign to define the limits of the Addict's realm, to give them order and structure. Addicts need the heroic Warrior to act in decisive ways and to cut through all the immobilizing entanglements that prevent Addicts from detaching from their gluttony for pleasure. And Addicts need the Seer to help them reflect, be objective, and see the bigger picture.[9] With the help of the other archetypes, the Addict can become a heroic Lover.

Addicts and Frigids are similar in their inability to make commitments, but for different reasons. Addicts cannot make commitments because they have *too much* energy, and so are perpetually restless. Frigids on the other hand cannot make commitments because they *lack* energy.

Frigid is a term traditionally applied to women, but I am applying it to men as well because it refers to those males and females who are completely divorced from the warmth of their own inner Lover. Lack of connection with their own emotions leaves Frigids without motive power. Frigids feel numb and in an emotional fog, unsure of what their real needs, desires, and feelings are. Without any vision, imagination, or passion, they feel internally joyless and dead.

Frigids are bored and boring, chronically depressed, and depressing to be around. They speak in monotones and display flat affect, that is, total listlessness and lack of enthusiasm. They feel cut off, uncommitted, and alienated from everyone, including themselves and loved ones, and they feel that nothing is worth doing — "all is vanity and chasing after the wind," as Ecclesiastes puts it.

Max Oliva outlines the many causes of male and female frigidity, which I will summarize. Some people don't know how to get close, and some are so wounded they can't get close. There are many reasons people fear intimacy: fear of losing your self, fear of being taken over by the other, fear of losing your identity, your life, your freedom, and fear of losing what you love. Sexuality can be distorted by feelings of being unlovable, lack of self-worth, guilt, repression, fear of abandonment, or of being overwhelmed by your own emotions or another's love, or fear of losing your vocation.

Blocks to intimacy, according to Oliva, include being out of touch with one's feelings; being betrayed when we trusted someone to honor our feelings; growing up in families where there was little intimacy, where the emotional growth of the parents and children was stunted; misreading signals from others, particularly regarding sex; feeling you need to be an authority figure to the other person and therefore are not able to be weak and vulnerable; being too established in your traditional role of teacher, leader, mother, or father to just be a friend; boredom in a relationship and just taking the other person for granted; differences in family background such as emotionally conflicted or distant parents; differences in culture, religion, or expectations; a poor self-image; emotional baggage from the past, and so on.[10]

Frigid people may have been taught at an early age that life is all about dominance, control, and outcompeting others. They learned that to have feelings is to be weak, that you cannot be vulnerable, or people will take advantage of you. They may have picked up the message that compassion encourages the poor to be dependent rather than self-reliant. Having suppressed all love and compassion, the Frigid can be like the Sadist.

Frigids may have been sexually abused as children, or may have grown up in a puritanical religious tradition that stifled sexual pleasure. They may be afraid of the body and its desires as temptations from the devil and a shortcut to hellfire. As teenagers, they may have been wounded by rejection and so, to prevent further pain, they numb out their Lover. As adults, they may be sexually inactive or have an unsatisfying sex life for a variety of reasons. Stress, depression, and financial problems can negatively impact sexual performance. Or they may feel bored with, angry at, or intimidated by their partner.

True Lovers honor sexuality and the body, but if Frigid persons believe that all sexual thoughts are sinful, they banish sexuality to the unconscious. When it surfaces later in Shadow forms such as a desire to be promiscuous or a fascination with pornography, they repress it further and thus put even more energy into the Shadow.

As their repressed sexuality gathers momentum underground, it may eventually explode as a volcano of sexual depravity: rape, child molestation, burning women at the stake as temptresses. Shadow Lovers often detest sexuality, but are possessed by lust. Many a fundamentalist Protestant, obsessed with preaching against the sins of the flesh, has been caught in adultery or with prostitutes. Solid moral teaching about sexuality is good, but the Catholic Church's strong teaching against sexual sin has not only not prevented sexual abuse, but, to the extent that it blocked priests from integrating sexuality into their lives, it may have actually caused hundreds of priests to abuse thousands of children. The healthy approach is not to repress sexual feelings into the Shadow, but to acknowledge their presence so you can make wise choices about them. Then you can consciously control your sexuality rather than having it subconsciously control you.

Carol Pearson describes well the twisted psychology of the Shadow Lover. Shadow Lovers sees themselves as machines, and other adults and children as targets. They are disconnected from their souls and the life-giving power of eros. They believe bodies are unclean and shameful, and sex is dirty. They dehumanize and objectify others so that they may be used as objects. Alienated from their own bodies, they are secretly jealous of those who have the life-force and energy they have lost. They project their repressed eroticism onto blacks and gays, and therefore oppress them.

According to Pearson, Shadow Lovers believe there is a spiritual hierarchy of love from eros to agape and that you have to give up eros for agape. They equate *chastity* with *celibacy*, and therefore believe that a person cannot be holy and sexually active. They see eros as egocentric and selfish, something to be suppressed, not affirmed and celebrated. Or they claim that agape, self-giving love, is the only acceptable Christian form of love, even though this is questionable biblically, theologically, and psychologically. Thus, they try to repress and kill eros to reach agape.[11]

Summing up, antiheroic Lovers as Addicts lack boundaries and so are enmeshed with everything, which results in a sense of lostness. They have lost their self and their soul in a swirl of pleasures. They are a glutton for pleasure and are never satisfied. They are out of control, live in chaos, and are the victim of their own sensitivity. They are jealous, envious, infatuated, narcissistic, undisciplined, restless, seductive, fragmented, and fickle. They cannot detach themselves from things, commit themselves to anything, or make long-range plans. They cannot delay gratification and so live for the sensuality of the moment.

Antiheroic Lovers as Frigids are repressed and sterile. Their life and affect are flat. They are numb, bored, listless, depressed, and unenthusiastic. Their life may feel unreal to them. They lack vision, imagination, and aliveness. They are disconnected from their soul and feelings and feel isolated from themselves, others, and God. They often try to get to agape by killing eros. They may detest the body and sexuality and see them as dirty or sinful and yet at the same time be secretly possessed by lust, since they project their repressed eroticism onto others. If they are sexually active at all, it is not tender, loving, or nurturing for them.

Chapter Six

HOW HEROIC SPIRITUAL GUIDES FORM HEROIC SEEKERS

What follows is a vision of the spiritual director or guide in a pure, ideal, and therefore heroic form, and so the spiritual directors presented here may seem larger than life. All the same, although they may be in the minority, there are in fact spiritual guides in every major religious tradition, both male and female, who approximate these ideal spiritual directors.

It is useful to state the ideal so that spiritual directors and guides have a high standard against which they can measure themselves. At the same time, perhaps the main part of being a good director or guide is the ability to love your real self and the real self of others. Therefore, good directors, while holding the ideal in mind, will not allow themselves to feel deflated if they do not reach the ideal. Rather they will intensify their efforts to love their real, human self.

Although each archetype of the spiritual director is unique, there is also considerable overlapping of qualities; every heroic archetype contains the other three, but to a lesser degree.

THE SOVEREIGN DIRECTOR

The heroic Sovereign is also a great Warrior, Seer, and Lover. The spiritual director as heroic Sovereign is therefore well-balanced, with the ability to bless, confront, transform, and love the directee.

The sense of the Sovereign Director's generativity and goodness will draw out the generativity and goodness of the directee. The Warrior in the Sovereign Director will help the directee form and defend spiritual boundaries, so that the directee is not overwhelmed by evil spirits or by fundamentalists. The discipline of the Warrior in the Sovereign Director will model for the directee how to resist temptation. The Seer in the Sovereign Director will facilitate directees in accessing the deepest spiritual recesses of their psyche, and the Lover in the Sovereign Director will help the directee savor and appreciate the richness and variety of people and of the whole creation.

The good Sovereign Director is selfless, always willing to go the extra mile with the directee and to be patient and gentle. Sovereign Directors do not get frustrated easily. They carry the directee's problems, when necessary, with appropriate dignity and gravity, and hand them back to the directee as the directee is ready to deal with them.

The Sovereign Director makes directees feel safe so that they can open up and share the inmost secrets of their soul. Directees know the Sovereign Director will accept whatever they say and never shame them. Whether or not Sovereign Directors *agree* with what directees share, they *accept* it as the valid experience of another human being.

The Sovereign Director is not threatened by any directee's power, social status, money, or education. Sovereign Directors feel comfortable with all directees, from all walks of life, whether rich or poor, educated or uneducated. They know that the uneducated are often more humble, of a deeper faith, and closer to God than the rich and powerful. They see the directee through God's eyes and know that the rich, from God's perspective, may be poor and blind and naked, even though they do not realize it.

Therefore, the Sovereign Director is compassionate toward the rich as well as toward the poor. The rich are relieved that they are accepted and not judged by the Sovereign Director, and therefore want to be like the Sovereign Director themselves, to be more heroic, compassionate, spiritual, and just. By the Sovereign Director's love, the rich are converted and want to share their wealth and use it for spiritual ends.

Sovereign Directors are models of authentic responsibility. They consider themselves to be important agents for the directee's spiritual growth and take their duties seriously, but they do not take responsibility for the directee's growth away from the directee. Directees are always given responsibility for their own process, but the Sovereign Director is there as the directee's helper and servant.

The Sovereign Director's responsibility to the directee is one of service, not ownership. The life of the directee belongs to the directee, not to the Sovereign Director. Therefore the Sovereign Director is *responsive to* the lives of directees, but not *responsible for* their lives. The responsibility of Sovereign Directors is to help directees in their growth process as best they can, without imposing anything. The Sovereign Director calls directees to their own sovereignty, that is, responsibility for and control over their own spiritual growth, to be the Sovereign of their own life, with the understanding that God is everyone's ultimate Sovereign.

The Sovereign Director gives the directee a sense of what emotional sturdiness is like. Since Sovereign Directors are emotionally stable, they are not easily shaken by what the directee says or does. The Sovereign Director is well grounded and rooted and can withstand the emotional storms of any directee. The Sovereign Director may need to give the male directee some worldly wisdom in order to bring him back to earth if the directee is floating around in his head or in the clouds like Peter Pan, the *puer eternus*, the *eternal boy*. The Sovereign Director may need to help both male and female directees be more realistic and to connect with their bodies, if their contemplation has become too ethereal.

The Sovereign Director can help directees make hard decisions. Sovereign Directors help the directee to do the best thing and the right thing, as hard as that may be at times. Sometimes directees have to go where they would not choose to go, if they are going to grow spiritually. They may have to confront sin or evil in their lives that they have been avoiding, because they know the confrontation will be very painful.

Since the Sovereign is the archetype of greatness, dignity, and self-possession, the Sovereign Director gives the directee a new vision of what a spiritually great human being could be like. From the Sovereign Director directees gain a new sense of being simultaneously more surrendered to God and more in possession of their own true self. They have a greater sense of their own spiritual dignity, their dignity in the eyes of God, since the Sovereign Director looks with kind eyes upon them.

Sovereign Directors keep their mind focused on what is noble and good and help the directee to do the same. Sovereign Directors generate a lot of ideas in their mind about what is happening in the directee's spiritual life and what the directee needs to do to grow, and they keep these ideas in mind as they listen to directees further explain their spiritual experiences. Sovereign Directors then select their own idea that best matches the directee's experience, and present it to the directee for verification. If Sovereign Directors are wrong, they are not shaken;

they simply listen more deeply and carefully to the directee. Like King Solomon, the Sovereign Director's constant prayer is for the wisdom to be a good director of people.

The heroic Sovereign Director is immensely organizing, ordering, and creatively healing. In the Sovereign Director's presence, directees gain a sense of right spiritual order, their lives feel more organized, and they feel more whole and healed. Learning to see reality through the Sovereign Director's eyes, directees feel that their lives have been enhanced and made fuller and richer. Directees sense the Sovereign Director's calmness and are restored to rationality. Their spiritual lives become more orderly and harmonious.

The Sovereign Director might become temporarily the center or anchor of directees' spiritual lives, until directees get their spiritual feet back on the ground, get rooted in reality again, and are able to become their own center again. The directee's center must ultimately be God, but the Sovereign Director can be a center outside the directee, until the directee is ready to find the center within, that is, God.

The Sovereign Director's office thus temporarily might be the one place in the world where directees feel safe, the one place from which directees can reconstruct their spiritual lives, the one place where directees can be freely creative, the one place from where the directee's creation radiates outward.

The Sovereign Director, rather than ordering directees to do anything, would simply help directees create the rules, guidelines, and values by which they organize and order their own spiritual lives. For example, the Sovereign Director might suggest that directees go to bed and get up half an hour earlier, so they can begin the day with meditation on the beatitudes or with centering prayer. The directee could then go through the day with the right values in mind, and in a centered and calm way.

The Sovereign Director understands, however, that directees know the fullness and all the circumstances and details of their own lives. The Sovereign Director knows only that fraction of the directee's life that is presented in the spiritual direction sessions. Therefore, Sovereign Directors understand that they are there to try to draw out directees' own wisdom about their own lives and that any suggestion the Sovereign Director makes is only a suggestion, one that directees can take home and meditate on, and decide if the suggestion makes sense, given all the details of their lives.

The Sovereign Director believes that Spirit works by way of *freedom*, and therefore suggestions given by the Sovereign Director will be genuinely helpful only if *freely* adopted by the directee. The Sovereign Director knows there is great power in the power of suggestion but never gets upset with the directee if the directee fails to adopt the Sovereign Director's recommendations.

If directees ask Sovereign Directors their opinion on something, Sovereign Directors are benevolent and authoritative, rather than authoritarian. They respect directees' freedom and leave them in charge of their own process. Again, they let directees be their own Sovereign.

The Christian Sovereign Director is the instrument by which God, the Sovereign Lord, passes on to the directee God's divine revelation, that is, Jesus Christ. The Sovereign Director not only suggests Bible verses to meditate on. More importantly, Sovereign Directors ground the directee in Jesus and invite the directee to discover anew how Jesus is revealing himself in the directee's life. So it is not a matter of converting directees to anything; it is rather a matter of helping directees discover how and where God is *already* active in their lives.

Sovereign Directors help directees discern the purpose and calling for their own realm, that is, the directee's own life. They help directees be clear about what is happening in their own lives and facilitate directees keeping focused on their own key spiritual issues.

Sovereign Directors who want their directees to grow spiritually must embody in themselves the spirit of their religious tradition, whatever the tradition is. Sovereign Directors must live the right order, the Eternal Way, and be a good example to directees. Good Sovereign Directors teach by example more than by word. They preach the gospel wherever they go, using words if necessary, as Francis of Assisi said. Sovereign Directors cannot be hypocrites, saying one thing and doing another. They must have a reputation for holiness. They must be righteous, without being self-righteous.

Sovereign Directors can expect rebellion from directees, or at least noncompliance, if they suggest that directees do something that Sovereign Directors do not do themselves. The directee is likely to throw back in the Sovereign Director's face, "But look at you. You don't live that way yourself, do you?" Sovereign Directors cannot truly facilitate order and righteousness in the directee's life if there is chaos and sin in their own life in the same area.

A Sovereign Director helps directees restore health, prosperity, and justice to their life, stop wrongdoing, and drive out evil. Sometimes Sovereign Directors have to activate their inner Warrior in order to mobilize the inner Warrior of the directee. They have to help the directee's Warrior enforce the slaying of the demons of chaos, sin, and death.

Sovereign Directors are spiritually fertile. Their primary role is to express the life-force, the libido of the cosmos, the love that comes from God, and thus beget many spiritual children. The Sovereign Director rains blessings upon directees at every appropriate opportunity, affirming and encouraging and blessing them in their walk with Spirit. This rain of blessings helps to loosen the hard-packed soil of the directee's soul, to massage it, and make it fecund again.

The Sovereign Director affirms and blesses directees just by meeting with them, being present to them, listening to them, looking on them with loving eyes, and accepting them, particularly when directees have exposed their soul, their innermost secrets, and all their warts and wounds and darkness to the director. The Sovereign Director blesses the directee by seeing and affirming the directee's true worth beneath all the wounds and sin.

Sovereign Directors admire and delight in directees. They shed God's grace on directees and make directees whole again by seeing directees with God's eyes. This helps directees to see themselves in a new light, that is, how they look to God. The main source of nonverbal information in human relations is our eyes. Our eyes can silently communicate so much. As representatives of God, Sovereign Directors, through their eyes, can literally show directees that God looks upon them with love.

Being seen, blessed, valued, listened to, and praised by the Sovereign Director heals directees and makes them whole, that is, it rightly orders their lives. The Sovereign Director knows how to create new life in others, how to make them grow in maturity. Sovereign Directors are comfortable with their own spirituality and not threatened by the spiritual growth of directees. Sovereign Directors are not jealous of, nor intimidated by, the spiritual giftedness of any directee. Rather they affirm, admire, and promote all directees' spiritual gifts.

The Sovereign Director always bows to and obeys God's greater wisdom. Sovereign Directors listen to the problems of the lowliest directee. They free the poor and helpless from their spiritual burden and take pity on the weakest human beings. Their genuine concern for their directees results in directees trusting Sovereign Directors unconditionally. The true Sovereign Director never violates this trust.

Directees love to be in the presence of Sovereign Directors. Every directee wants an audience with them, to be praised and validated by them. Directees consider their sessions with the Sovereign Director to be very important, and they rearrange the rest of their lives so they can be there. In the Sovereign Director's presence, the directee feels completely understood and accepted.

Sovereign Directors activate their inner Warrior to protect their own boundaries, so that their inner and outer life is not overrun with the stress of their spiritual direction practice. While their Warrior may tell them to go the extra mile with a particular directee, their Warrior also tells them not to over-book appointments with directees, to contain sessions within a one-hour limit, and to rest or escape when they have absorbed too much negativity from directees who are in spiritual chaos. Sovereign Directors also activate the fun, laughter, and play of their inner Lover to keep their life in balance and to prevent overseriousness. On the other hand, if they are too comfortable and their spiritual growth is grinding to a halt, Sovereign Directors activate their inner Seer in order to keep learning.

As mentioned earlier, Sovereign Directors are down to earth, and accept the world as it is. They do not have their head in the clouds, nor are they squeamish about the realities of the ordinary material world. Sovereign Directors know how to get their needs met and enjoy expressing themselves in the physical domains of work, home, and financial management.

Sovereign Directors are not dualists: they do not separate spirit and body or locate the directee's or their own spiritual fulfillment in some other realm than the ordinary workaday world. They invite the directee to be realistic about the monetary and energy demands of family life. They help directees discern what is *enough* material prosperity for their particular life situation, so that directees live in neither poverty nor excess. Sovereign Directors help directees live in our consumer culture with detachment and voluntary simplicity, while meeting the basic physical needs of themselves and their loved ones.

Sovereign Directors give directees the wisdom to swim against the cultural current of materialism by suggesting they follow the Buddhist Middle Path of moderation in all things, or by reminding them of Christ's dictum to store up treasure in heaven. And the Spirit of God, working through the Sovereign Director, gives directees the strength to conquer the waterfall of money by keeping their eyes on heavenly rather than earthly rewards.

Sovereign Directors are realists. They have no illusions about the reality of evil and so teach their directees to guard against it. They also have no illusions about themselves. Good Sovereign Directors know their own Shadow and take responsibility for it, so their Shadow does not interfere with the spiritual direction sessions or get passed on subconsciously to the directee. Sovereign Directors have the humility to see when they are becoming a dogmatic Tyrant or a wounded Abdicator. In either case, they know where to go to get the healing they need.

While respecting confidentiality, Sovereign Directors consult with wise advisers if they are having difficulty with a directee; in other words, they call upon the Seer in others. They avoid making decisions about a directee simply on the basis of their own ego-needs, whims, or subjective perceptions. Rather, with the directee's permission, they consult doctors, psychologists, and social workers, if necessary. They also listen to their soul and their own deepest feelings and intuitions about the directee, that is, they access their own inner Seer.

Heroic Sovereign Directors keep in mind the collective common good when meeting with a directee. In other words, they keep in mind the directee's family and social groups, churches, mosques, synagogues, and other communities the directee belongs to, and they consider the impact the spiritual direction session may have on these other people through the directee. Sovereign Directors create a better life, not just for the directee, but also for all those whose lives are touched by the directee.

Although they could become wealthy by manipulating directees, good Sovereign Directors avoid this temptation by living simply in an ethical relationship to money. Their royal presence and ability to inspire the directee does not depend on wealth or show of any kind. Sovereign Directors have conquered the waterfall of monetary temptations themselves, by the power of the Spirit working in them.

Sovereign Directors consider spiritual direction to be a royal task and know that every Sovereign Director fails at this task at some point. They know that they will be confronted with their own powerlessness in the face of suffering, and with their own smallness in contrast to both the power of evil and the power of God. They know the only solution is to surrender to God and to claim the small amount of power and ability God has given them in a humble and healthy way. If they accept their own weakness and woundedness, God can do great things through Sovereign Directors. When they recognize their own human fallibility and see the Sovereign archetype at work in others, they stop trying to do everything by themselves and lose any desire to lord it over anyone.

Heroic Sovereign Directors do not stifle conflict. Rather, they handle it in a productive way so there is harmony and order. They understand and appreciate the gifts of people very different from themselves and find ways to help them use their gifts productively. They do not blame or exclude those who are weak or selfish, nor make excuses for them; rather they struggle with them to find their gifts and purpose.

True Sovereign Directors seek to live in alignment with the will of God and their own deepest inner wisdom. They offer their suffering up as a sacrifice to the Higher Power and surrender the reins of power to God. As they surrender all narcissism and the self-serving ego, God empowers them to become ever greater Sovereign Directors. As they let go and let God be the Director of the spiritual direction sessions more and more, things become easier and go well in a miraculous way.

For Christians, Jesus Christ best shows us what the true Sovereign Director is like. Since he is Prophet (Warrior), Priest (Seer), King (Sovereign), and Lover, Christ shows us how to fulfill the four heroic archetypes all in one. Like Christ, the Sovereign Director refuses to bow to Satan when tempted to rule over other people's lives.

Without ego-inflation, Sovereign Directors graciously accept any adulation directees shower upon them, pointing the directees to God as the true source of their sovereign power. They know in their hearts that all their goodness and ability as directors is a gift from God, and they would have no power at all if it didn't come from above.

True Sovereign Directors don't allow directees to make them into Sovereigns for their own political purposes. They refuse to become instruments of anyone's warped agenda. They are committed to justice as integral to spirituality but keep directees focused on the spirituality underlying politics rather than on politics per se. On the other hand, the Sovereign Director is wary of those New Age approaches that advocate mysticism without justice.

True Sovereign Directors never exploit the power of their role. They are interested in service, not power, status, or money. They never ask their directees to abandon their rationality, responsibility, or autonomy. Sovereign Directors do not make it easy for directees by asking them to hand their lives over to the Sovereign Director. Like Jesus, they encourage their directees to become like children instead of seeking power. They eschew the pagan style of authority, that is, lording it over others. To change people's lives, they use attraction rather than force, elicit love not fear, model service not domination.

Also like Jesus, the Sovereign Director does not dither, avoid thorny issues, or compromise with evil. Sovereign Directors stand against political or religious expediency. They speak the truth and do not let religious authorities manipulate them. Their authority is direct and clear and rests upon their wisdom, integrity, and holiness. They ask nothing of their directees that they do not ask of themselves. Their only goal for directees is that directees love God totally and love others as themselves, much as Sovereign Directors try to do themselves.

Sovereign Directors, like Jesus, exhibit internal nobility and psychic greatness even though they have none of the trappings of institutional power. Even as priests in some backwater parish or laypersons unacknowledged by their religious hierarchy, still their inner Sovereign shines forth. Particularly when they are going through a dark night of the soul and feel abandoned by God, their royal greatness of spirit keeps them centered in God and faithful to God. They know that God is with them because they know that their own faithfulness is God's gift to them, whether they feel God's presence or not. Their desire to be with God is, in fact, God working in them and not abandoning them. Even though God might slay them, still will they trust in the Lord. As Job said, "Let God kill me if God wills it, I still have no hope except in God" (Job 13:15).

The directee learns this unconditional trust from the Sovereign Director, either verbally or nonverbally. Directees also become more realistic, centered, and grounded in the Spirit of God. Their lives become better ordered and emotionally stable, clearly focused and purposeful in their pursuit of the reign of God. They feel loved, blessed, valued, and affirmed by God. They are better able to integrate their body and the material, workaday world into their spiritual lives. They feel empowered to bring new life, service, and justice to others. They feel freer of sin and compulsion and their own Shadow. They are much more aware of their own dignity and nobility as children of a Sovereign God and become more and more heroic Sovereigns in their own lives.

THE WARRIOR DIRECTOR

Spiritual directors as heroic Warriors commit themselves to a mighty cause: that everyone become a lover of God. They fight against the powers of darkness, nothingness, and destruction so prevalent in our culture. They fight for light and life, and they are willing to give up their own convenience and comfort and sacrifice everything so that others might grow spiritually.

The Warrior Director is the most challenging of the heroic directors for the directee to work with. In the presence of a Warrior Director, directees know they have a powerful ally on their side in the fight against evil. Directees know they are loved, but it is with an unemotional, no-nonsense, tough love. They immediately intuit that the Warrior Director is committed to their good. Warrior Directors quickly gain the directee's respect.

The goal of the heroic Warrior Director is either the destruction of evil in the directee's life or to make a life-enhancing difference for the directee through struggle. Warrior Directors fear powerlessness and ineptitude on their part, that is, that they won't reach the directee's heart and slay the evil that exists there. The gifts of the Warrior Director are courage and discipline.

Warrior Directors fight for what really matters but they are not aggressive. The aggressive director invades the directee's life, without any respect for the directee's boundaries. The passive director listens but does not confront the directee and therefore does not access the directee's deeper issues. Directees sometimes need to be confronted because their ego erects massive barriers to prevent its own spiritual transformation. Heroic Warrior Directors are assertive, not aggressive or passive, that is, they know their own needs and the needs of the directee, and they meet the needs of both. Directees need to be challenged without being violated, to be confronted, to have their barriers broken through, but with tact and skill. The primary need of Warrior Directors is to fulfill their task as spiritual directors, that is, to fulfill the spiritual growth of the directee.

Directees feel safe with the Warrior Director as their ally. They feel protected from evil, and they know the Warrior Director will respect them and not violate them in any way. On the other hand, they also know that they cannot easily deceive the Warrior Director. The Warrior Director will cut right through the underbrush, the camouflage, the defense mechanisms, and the obfuscations and go right to the heart of the matter at hand. With the help of the Warrior Director, the directee is empowered to confront, perhaps for the first time, issues that were formerly avoided or hidden.

The heroic Warrior Director avoids ruthlessness, the unprincipled and obsessive need to "win," that is, to persuade directees that their religious experience is wrong, and that they must approach spirituality the way the director does. Warrior Directors are not interested in conquest, nor do they see differences as a threat. They encourage the uniqueness of each directee. Directees feel that their religious experience, whatever it is, is valued and validated by the Warrior Director. Directees feel that they can just be themselves and open up to the Warrior Director in complete safety.

Warrior Directors have confronted spiritual challenges, obstacles, and demons within themselves and defeated them by calling upon the power, grace, and wisdom of God. Warrior Directors are very aware of their own Shadow, their areas of weakness and temptation, and are constantly on guard against them. They know their greatest enemy is themselves, and so they maintain a deep prayer life.

Directees feel that there are no demons, temptations, or weaknesses in their own life that Warrior Directors will not confront, and have not wrestled with themselves, and so they cannot shock or surprise the Warrior Director. Knowing the Warrior Director will not be scandalized or disgusted, no matter how horrible their sins, directees feel free to be completely real with the Warrior Director.

The Warrior Director is always alert because it takes clear thinking to discern how much assertiveness is appropriate given the changing circumstances in the directee's life. Warrior Directors focus their minds and bodies in the session to get results. They want to help their directees to *be all they can be* in spirit, soul, thoughts, feelings, speech, and actions. Warrior Directors are mindful, that is, always aware of what is happening. They are strategists and tacticians of spiritual growth. They know what they want, that is, the deepened spirituality of the directee, and they know how to get it. They realistically assess the strengths, skills, limits, and weaknesses of themselves and the directee.

From the Warrior Director directees learn how to focus their spiritual quest and to always be alert, for they know not when their death, or their Lord, will come. They learn to "Be awake!" as both Jesus and the Buddha said. They become more aware of their Shadows and temptations. They will not be caught off guard like the foolish virgins in Matthew 25.

Directees learn to heed the words of Ephesians 6:11–12: "Put on the armor of God.... For our struggle is not with flesh and blood." From the Warrior Director's study of Ignatius of Loyola and Teresa of Avila, directees come to understand the spiritual warfare tactics of evil spirits, for example, attacking us where we are most vulnerable spiritually. If a directee has a temptation with regard to alcohol or lust or greed, that is where an evil spirit will mount its strongest offensive. Directees also become mindful of the words of Peter: "Be sober and vigilant. Your opponent the devil is prowling around like a roaring lion looking for someone to devour" (1 Pet 5:8).

Warrior Directors know how fast or slow to go with the directee. They are flexible and shift tactics if an approach is not working. If they believe a directee is headed for spiritual desolation, Warrior Directors challenge the directee. Warrior Directors are spiritually confident, for they know that to doubt is to lose the spiritual battle. If directees are heading for spiritual consolation and growth, the Warrior Director cheers them on and encourages them.

Warrior Directors live in the Eternal Now, the only place where God is found. Their constant awareness of their own possibly imminent death makes them focus upon the present moment and creates a desire in them to make every action and word count. Possible shortness of life means they do not hesitate. They take immediate decisive action and engage the directee head on. They think, but they do not think too much or too long.

From the Warrior Director directees learn the preciousness of every moment. They learn not to regret or glorify the past, nor to fear or get overly excited about the future, but to live calmly and fully in the reality of the Eternal Now that is God.

Warrior Directors' responses to the directee are unconscious reflex actions trained for through enormous self-discipline in spiritual reading and through extensive spiritual direction sessions with past directees. Their responses are skillful, powerful, and accurate.

Warrior Directors have great self-control, both inner and outer, psychological and physical. They are very aware how they are communicating nonverbally. They do not let their own issues, fears, or grief leak through into their nonverbal behavior. Warrior Directors may strongly disagree with a directee's choices or values, but they do not show their disagreement nonverbally or verbally, unless they feel it is appropriate to do so. Otherwise, they file their disagreement in the back of their mind and bring it up at a more strategic time. Directees feel free to be themselves but know that they will be tactfully confronted if the Warrior Director feels they are getting too far off track or endangering their spiritual progress.

Warrior Directors conserve their energy, and they never overdo things. They never fight over trivial issues. They never talk in the session more than is necessary. They are a master of "weapons" (tools such as the Myers Briggs Type Indicator or the Enneagram), which they use efficiently to reach their goal.

Warrior Directors are a study in trained self-control, first of all, of their own minds and attitudes. Their attitude is always positive; they have an unconquerable spirit and great courage. They are fearless and take responsibility for their own actions.

Directees, through the example and mentoring of the Warrior Director, learn greater self-control as well. They learn to do what is humanly possible and to leave the humanly impossible up to God, knowing that God specializes in the impossible. Like the Warrior Director, the directee learns to think clearly about what is possible and what is impossible.

The Warrior Director's self-discipline includes the ability to absorb and withstand great emotional pain coming from directees. Since Warrior Directors are disciplined with their own fear, anger, and sadness, they can handle that of directees. They are willing to suffer hardship to achieve their goals with the directee. They are willing to travel into deep suffering with the directee, never abandoning the directee in the journey, and always being there when the going gets rough and the directee needs them.

Unafraid of suffering of any kind, whether physical, emotional, or spiritual, Warrior Directors are willing and able to accompany the directee into the darkest night of the soul. When directees are walking through the Valley of the Shadow of Death, they know that they are not alone. For "the Lord is a warrior" (Exod 15:3) at their side, and so is their spiritual director.

The Warrior Director's transpersonal commitment is to God and God's reign; the Warrior Director is loyal to God even unto death. This transpersonal commitment relativizes all personal relationships, so that relationships are less central than this commitment. Since their whole psyche is organized around their central commitment to God, Warrior Directors eliminate all petty ego concerns. It is only out of commitment to God, never out of ego, that the Warrior Director is willing to kill, or at least prune off, whatever needs to be pruned or killed for the directee to grow spiritually.

For example, Warrior Directors would ask directees to try to eliminate any sin, corruption, injustice, or obsolete rituals from their spiritual life. Like Paul of Tarsus, they would ask directees to live a life worthy of the calling to which they have been called, to fight the good fight, to discipline themselves in every way, for they are striving not for a transient laurel wreath as the Greek athletes do, but for an eternal crown.

Warrior Directors also would help directees discern whether they need to leave their job or change their lifestyle if it is unfulfilling and help them find the courage to do so. In short, the Warrior Director helps directees eliminate whatever no longer serves them. God does the same for us. God prunes and disciplines those God loves (Heb 12:6), which is all of us. Thus, directees grow in purity, self-discipline, courage, and self-confidence, if they do what God and the Warrior Director suggest.

Warrior Directors pray to Yahweh, the Warrior-God, to Michael, the Warrior-angel, or to Joan of Arc, the Warrior-saint, to help them resist temptation and fight this holy war against the powers of evil and idolatry. If they are Christians, they align themselves with Christ, as leader of the forces of light, against Satan, the lord of chaos and darkness. Christian Warrior Directors and their directees know clearly which side of the Two Standards (described by Ignatius of Loyola in the *Spiritual Exercises*) they are on. On the battlefield of life, they gather under the banner of Christ, where there is peace, joy, and love, and not under the banner of Satan, where rebellion, despair, and hatred rule.

The heroic Warrior Director, unalloyed by the other archetypes, is emotionally distant and detached without being cruel. Emotional detachment allows Warrior Directors to think clearly about directees without getting their own issues tangled up in their perceptions of what is happening in the directees' lives and what the directees need. Warrior Directors look at the directee's whole case dispassionately and objectively and then act forcefully, efficiently, and swiftly, with their own ego and personal feelings out of the way. Directees likewise learn to look at their own lives objectively. They let go of their ego, their petty likes and dislikes, more and more.

Emotional detachment can make the Warrior Director seem unavailable. However, when connected to the Sovereign energy, the Warrior Director stewards the realm (their spiritual direction practice) not only with decisiveness, clarity, discipline, and courage, but also with generativity and creativity. And, when the Lover is activated, the Warrior Director can, while dispassionately helping the directee battle temptation and sin, also have a sense of compassion for humans struggling in all their frailty. Connection with the Seer allows the Warrior Director to channel God's healing power to the directee. The inner Seer and inner Sovereign tell the Warrior Director which battles are worth fighting and which are not. The well-rounded Warrior Director enables directees to access their Lover, Sovereign, and Seer as well.

Warrior Directors who have activated their Lover archetype fight the good fight for justice and freedom, not just out of commitment to God's will, but also out of love for their brothers and sisters. On the other hand, there is no true love without the sword. For example, faithful spouses must cut themselves off from other women and men, and directors and directees, out of love of God, must cut themselves off from any evil influences.

The Warrior Director helps directees to activate their own inner Warrior so that they can set and defend their own spiritual boundaries against the spiritually violent consumer culture we live in, where people compete and fight for the Great Idol, the Almighty Dollar. The Warrior Director helps directees to distinguish between who they are before God, versus what has been culturally programmed into them by corporate capitalism. As Francis of Assisi said, who we are is who we are in the eyes of God, nothing more or less.

Warrior Directors delight in danger, in wrestling with the forces of evil. They are characterized by single-mindedness and fortitude in spiritual direction sessions. They do not jump from issue to issue with directees, but after asking the directee what they want to talk about that day, they take the directee's main issue or experience and explore it in depth, not being afraid to go wherever an issue leads them. Directees feel satisfied that the issue of the day was thoroughly dealt with in the spiritual direction session.

Warrior Directors know their limits. They know when to say "yes" when taking on a challenging directee, and when to decline. Warrior Directors know how to use their energy and harness their reserves — emotional, mental, physical, and spiritual. They conserve energy for arduous parts of the journey so they can go the distance with their directees and not get burned out.

Warrior Directors know that not every directee will like or accept them. They know that in spiritual direction some directees do not want to know the truth, even when the director speaks it with compassion. Warrior Directors have the courage to be different and not just go with the flow of popular opinion. They dare to stand for moral values, ethical behavior, and justice, and to resist the pressure to conform to the lowest common standards. They have integrity and a strong conscience, brave disapproval, and fight for what they believe is right, with honesty and fairness toward others and loyalty toward God. They do all this with tact and a nonjudgmental, nonself-righteous attitude.

Warrior Directors do not deny or simply endure their own negative feelings; they integrate them. They integrate their anger and express it appropriately and assertively in the spiritual direction session, as Jesus did in confronting the hypocrisy of the Pharisees. They combine honesty with tactfulness, that is, they speak the truth with love, as St. Paul advocated. They know that if they repress their negative emotions too much, rather than integrating them, they will eventually express them in inappropriate and destructive ways. When they inadvertently do something destructive, they are humble enough to apologize.

Warrior Directors keep a positive attitude and focus on the good in life, and in the directee. They do not let their own trials and calamities grind them down, nor those of the directee. They strive constantly for their goal of the directee's spiritual growth and know how deeply embedded a directee's issues can be. Therefore, they are willing to go over and over an issue with a directee, no matter how repetitive it is, until the directee experiences liberation. Directees deeply appreciate the Warrior Director's patience with them.

The good Warrior Director has high ideals about the reign of God, and is willing to take risks to defend weak directees and protect them from harm. The Warrior Director helps the directee stand up to Tyrants and other oppressors who use their authority unfairly. The Warrior Director treats all directees with

respect, and fights to ennoble them, particularly the poor. Warrior Directors are very aware of the reality of evil and assertively
confront it, while at the same time never emotionally hurting
others unnecessarily. They always use the least force necessary
to protect the directee's boundaries.

Two of the Warrior Director's tactics are secrecy and strategic
retreat. Secrecy is about camouflage, and not entering battles
until you are well-prepared for them. As was said earlier, Warrior
Directors camouflage their nonverbal reactions to the directee,
gather more information from the directee (which could take
months), get totally prepared, and raise the issue only when
they know it is worth the risk.

Warrior Directors know about smart fighting. They know
where and when to fight, and they are wise enough to back
off if overwhelmed with the directee's spiritual problems. If
the directee inadvertently brings up the director's own unre-
solved issue, the director may need to take extra time away
from the spiritual direction sessions to work on that issue with
a counselor, nurse wounds, heal, rebuild strength, think over
how to attack the directee's issue, bide time, learn new combat or conflict resolution skills, and wait for the right opening
before engaging that particular issue with the directee again.

Smart Warrior Directors can rapidly identify directees who
will be difficult opponents. They quickly discern a directee's
Myers Briggs or Enneagram type and fight accordingly, using a
different strategy for each type. Warrior Directors quickly identify obstacles to spiritual growth and think of how to overcome
them, using the strengths and weaknesses in their directees.
They listen carefully to the directee and adjust their strategies
and battle plan, but not their goal. They relentlessly pursue the
directee's spiritual growth.

Actual verbal combat with the directee is the choice of last resort, after the Warrior Director has thought through and tried all other options. Warrior Directors prefer peace and harmony in the spiritual direction relationship but do not fear conflict. The most skillful Warrior Directors may battle mainly with their own wits outside of the direction session, studying various approaches and what is likely to work with different personality types.

The wise Warrior Director knows when to admit defeat and refer the directee to someone else with more expertise in a particular area. Warrior Directors learn from their defeats and failures. They intelligently assess people and situations and try to discern what is best not only for the directee, but also all those they might affect. Their strong personal values and wisdom tell them which aspects of the directee need the most attention. However, if their strategy does not work, they take it in their stride, learn from it, and move on with different tactics. Warrior Directors are not paralyzed by lack of success, nor overly attached to any one method of relating to directees. They know a wide variety of spiritual techniques.

Since Warrior Directors focus on the goal more than on people, they can keep a cool, objective head in the midst of stress and interpersonal tension. The struggle brings out the best in Warrior Directors. They value independence and achievement for the directee, primary values of our culture. However, Warrior Directors are not committed to the status quo by any means. They keep justice, peace, and a vision of a better world always in front of them. They benefit society by forming Warrior Directees who are independent of our culture, where our culture's values are not life-giving, and goal-oriented enough to fight for peace and justice until they win.

The real battle for Warrior Directors is always against the enemy within themselves: their own Shadow in the form of sloth, cynicism, fear, grief, bitterness, despair, irresponsibility, denial, and so on. Warrior Directors confront these inner demons and emotional pains with courage, self-discipline, and skill, trying always to find wisdom, and to see the connections between all things as well as balancing their Warrior values with those of the other three archetypes.

Directees learn from Warrior Directors how to battle evil within and outside themselves in a heroic way, when to fight for their spiritual growth and when to let God take over, how to integrate suffering into their lives, stay focused on God and their mission in hard times, stand up for what they believe in, fight smart, be objective, learn from defeat, and be totally committed to God's cause.

THE SEER DIRECTOR

The Seer is the natural archetype of the spiritual director.

The goal of Seers is transformation of lesser into better realities; their fear is folly; their response to a problem is to transform or heal it; their task is alignment of their true self with the cosmos; and their gift is personal power.

Based on the above, the goal of heroic Seer Directors is transformation of the directee's spiritual reality; their fear is the directee's folly, that is, having the directee turn away from God; their response to a spiritual roadblock in the directee is to help the directee transform or heal it (e.g., transforming the directee's image of God from Tyrant to blessing Sovereign). The task of Seer Directors is to align themselves and the directee with God, so that God becomes the true spiritual director in their sessions. The gift of the Seer Director is spiritual empowerment of the directee.

More than with any other archetypal director, the directee can spiritually grow under the influence of the Seer Director. Directees are particularly empowered to deal with their Shadow, to step into their personal subconscious and collective unconscious, to heal any psychospiritual wounds that are lying dormant there, as well as to name and claim their golden Shadow, the psychospiritual gifts the directee has hidden, repressed, or denied.

Seer Directors often have to realize their own personal powerlessness through spiritual combat with demons of addiction, illness (physical or emotional), or disaster, before their ego can give up its grip and they can fully surrender to God. Through weakness, they learn the humility necessary to let God be the Sovereign in every aspect of their life. Only at this point do Seer Directors fully have an authentic spiritual direction ministry. Through total conversion, they have earned the right to be called a spiritual director. However, Seer Directors who are not yet totally surrendered to God may also know that they have been called to this ministry, and called to further surrender, because they have constantly recurring visions, synchronistic experiences, consolations, or intuitions that this is God's will for them.

Seer Directors know, from personal experience with their own demons and aspirations, how to heal directees and how to help them reflect on their visions and dreams. They know how to help directees ground their inspirations and make them real through action. They help directees make dreams come true. The Seer Director knows that everything is interconnected, and that directees can change their physical circumstances by changing their mental, emotional, and spiritual realities.

Directees find that, with the help of the Seer, they are able to shift into a new paradigm of reality, putting spiritual things first and trusting that as long as they are faithful to this, everything else will be taken care of, as Jesus promised (Matt 6:33). This frees directees to live their dreams, to follow their bliss, knowing that money, or whatever else they need, will follow.

Seer Directors know the processes and stages of transformation and spiritual growth and how to initiate directees from one spiritual stage to another. They keep initiating spiritual novices by helping them progress through Teresa of Avila's inner mansions, until they are mature mystics. Initiation from one level or stage to another involves showing directees, or helping them to understand in an ever deeper way, their own powerlessness and ever deepening need of God.

The Seer Director helps directees uncover their spiritual wounds, wounds inflicted by God that can be healed only by greater faith and trust in God's grace and unconditional love. Spiritual wounds from God, which are really an invitation to deeper faith, explain the common occurrence among charismatics and others strongly dedicated to God of their faith suddenly drying up and the sweet consolation they had always known suddenly disappearing so they feel they are now in a spiritual desert. It explains someone as devout as Mother Teresa of Calcutta feeling abandoned by God. It explains Christ's cry on the cross "My God, my God, why have you forsaken me?" (Matt 27:46).

John of the Cross has written extensively about this kind of dark night of the soul. Quite simply, it is easier to believe when everything is going well and you directly feel or sense God's presence and love and protection at every turn in the road. When all that vanishes, faith is not so effortless, but God is just challenging us to no longer base our faith on *feelings*, but on an act of the *will*. If we can develop this kind of faith, we can withstand any kind of trial and become a true spiritual hero, with a faith that is unshakeable, the kind of faith Mother Teresa had. So out of love and out of desire for our development, God sometimes hides from us, or *wounds* us, by taking away all our consolations, as happened with Job in the Hebrew scriptures. Job was faced with a choice: either give up, curse God, and spiritually die, or develop an unconditional trust in God, the kind of trust that says, "Even if I feel abandoned by God, or even if God lets me die, I will still trust in God." This is the kind of faith that Job had and that Jesus had on the cross.

Seer Directors are themselves initiates — by study and by their own experiences — into knowledge that seems secret and hidden because the average disciple has not had the time, energy, resources, interest, or inclination to investigate it. Thus, the heroic Seer Director is well versed in theology, scripture, methods of prayer, and writings of the mystics.

The Seer Director is also a keen observer of God's creation and all the spiritual lessons to be gleaned from the natural world. The natural world was God's original revelation and scripture before there were any holy books. The Seer Director is in touch with nature, and how everything in it — thunder and lightning, strange animals and birds, rain and rainbows, the sun and moon — can point us to God. The Seer archetype is the archetype of awareness, and therefore the Seer Director can help the directee awaken to the natural world and its limitless possibilities.

Under the guidance of the Seer Director, directees find themselves living in harmony with nature and with the thrust of evolution toward higher and higher states of consciousness. Directees also find, as they connect in a deeper way with the natural world, that they become more concerned about ecological issues, and more inclined to speak out about environmental degradation. They start to see for themselves the impending environmental apocalypse.

The people of God go to the Seer Director with their spiritual questions, their spiritual deserts, their spiritual sufferings, in the hope of finding truth and meaning. Seer Directors listen to their confessions, the deep dark secrets of their souls, and through their insight, intuition, and experience help directees foresee the future of their life if they travel down various paths. With the grace of God, the Seer Director and the directee can foretell what the consequences of various choices are likely to be.

The intimate knowledge of God and God's ways that Seer Directors have gives them great spiritual power. The people of God hold Seer Directors in great respect and reverence. Seer Directors often advise spiritual leaders such as rabbis, ministers, priests, and bishops. The health and survival of the people of God depend on wise Seer Directors as much as on their spiritual leaders.

Seer Directors change directees' reality by changing their consciousness, and they change directees' consciousness by radiating God's love, acceptance, and peace to the directee. Seer Directors are holy and thus send out healing vibrations without effort. They are full of the presence of God, so that when Seer Directors appear, evil spirits flee.

Directees, in the presence of the Seer Director, get a new sense of holiness, become more holy themselves, and all the virtues grow in them. They become more moral, not on the basis of legalities and rule following, but on the basis of feeling loved by God through the Seer Director and desiring to please God as a result.

The Seer Director gives the directee a sense of unity, of connection with the whole, the understanding that the *inner* contains and creates the *outer,* and that God is *within* us, in our minds and hearts, not just *out there*. The Spirit dwells most powerfully in the collective unconscious with the archetypes, and so Seer Directors help directees unite the conscious and unconscious minds. They help directees get their ego out of the way so that God can flow through the directee and change the world. They also help directees understand how God has called them, gifted them with various fruits of the Spirit, various charisms and powers, and is sending them out to transform society.

Seer Directors facilitate directees reading the signs of the times, and the signs in their own lives, the synchronicity that points the way directees should go. They assist directees in trusting God's wisdom, that God will send them the right people and resources just when they need them. They help directees go with the flow of God's truth and grace rather than the flow of secular culture, which is often at odds with truly spiritual values. They aid directees in integrating God's will and their own soul's purpose, that is, to love God with all their heart and their neighbor as themselves. They support directees in seeing that their own deepest desire can also be God's desire for them.

Seer Directors awaken the Seer archetype within themselves through meditation, prayer, or guided fantasy. They consciously enter the right brain and collective unconscious and receive from them guidance, wisdom, and energy. Through their imagination they consult with their inner Seer or confront a problem as if it were a dragon. They teach directees how to do all this, so that directees might find their own answers. Seer Directors trust their own inner voices, intuitive insights, dreams, fantasies, and even their extrasensory perceptions, all of which are the Spirit's ways of giving them psychic foreshadowings of events in the directee's life. Seer Directors often find that outside of the spiritual direction session new revelations and insights come to them about particular directees.

Male Seer Directors are sensitive to their *anima*, the feminine aspect of their psyche, and therefore can guide male directees beyond exploitation of women and Mother Earth. On directed retreats, they guide men by their example to a greater integration of the masculine and feminine, the rational and the intuitive, courage and wisdom. They show men the way of love for the feminine, which includes respect, patience, listening, and surrender to God.

Seer Directors do not hesitate to share their secret knowledge when they deem it wise and appropriate to do so. They compassionately judge what the directee is capable of understanding and adjust their responses accordingly. They use their expertise to serve the good of others. They do not overcharge for their services or make directees feel stupid for their lack of knowledge. They serve the directee rather than serving themselves through the pursuit of money or prestige. They use their gifts prudently for the healthy integration of the directee. They know the overwhelming power of archetypes and help directees arouse them in their psyche, and then they regulate and channel their energy flow.

Directees trust the Seer Director because they know the Seer Director will let them go at their own pace, so they are not overwhelmed with more than they can handle. Directees sense new energy and aliveness growing within themselves, but in a nonthreatening way.

The special gift of Seer Directors is to think clearly, to make complex and difficult decisions and judgments with careful deliberation. They are thoughtful, reflective, aware, and insightful. They are masters of Ignatius of Loyola's *Rules for*

Discerning God's Will and *Rules for Discerning Spirits.* They can detach from inner and outer storms and connect to deep inner truths, wisdom, and resources. Their detachment makes them stable, and not easily pulled or pushed around by a directee's ups and downs. Their steadiness helps the directee calm down and become more centered. The Seer Director's centeredness allows the directee to weigh the options and possible outcomes more reasonably. Seer Directors convey God's grace to the directee under pressure.

Seer Directors are astute observers, and this gives them deep understanding of people. Their technical skill in containing and channeling the psychological and spiritual forces of themselves and others allows them to transform the directee's black magic (wild, chaotic emotions) into white magic (useful actions). Directees have a sense of being more surrendered to God, yet more in control of their life, by the grace of God. As directees progressively give themselves to God, God gives them their true self back more and more. Obedience to God is thus liberating, not enslaving.

Heroic Seer Directors welcome the Sovereign archetype's concern for generativity and generosity, the Warrior archetype's ability to act decisively and with courage, and the Lover archetype's deep connectedness to all things. Seer Directors thus integrate the other archetypes well, which results in using their knowledge, containment, and channeling of energy for the good of all directees.

As directees come into greater contact with the heroic archetypes in all their purity and interconnectedness, they become not only more heroic Seers, but also more heroic Sovereigns, Warriors, and Lovers.

Seer Directors are tuned in to the many ways God speaks to us, inside and out. Their intuitive right brain is open to the vast storehouse of the personal subconscious and the collective unconscious. They thus often know instinctively what the directee needs to do, without being able to pinpoint how they know. In a situation of great ambiguity, they thus can help the directee make the right decision, which brings inner peace.

Seer Directors identify with the hopes, dreams, fears and longings of others, and this allows them to interpret others' thoughts, feelings, motives, and moods. They help people to heal by bringing out of their unconscious forgotten and hurtful memories that are still inhibiting them, or idolatrous identifications that trap them in negativity or sin.

Seer Directors have the power of *naming* and therefore can liberate directees from the perceptions of others and their internalized voices, which are often abusive. They help directees find out who they truly are by helping them see themselves through God's eyes. Then directees can replace their "I'm a God-forsaken sinner" tape with "I am a beloved child of God." Seer Directors empower directees by naming them "contemplative" rather than "slothful." They change directees' identities by helping them see that they are not an "old man" or "old woman," but a "sage" or "crone," which implies a privileged status involving wisdom, mentoring, and guidance of the young.

Along with a new self-image, directees gain greater clarity about the purpose of their lives and greater freedom from past sins. Seer Directors also help directees transform their lives by aiding them in seeing the opportunities in problems and the learning in mistakes. They help them see gifts in seemingly negative things.

Just as a shaman would exorcise demons, the Seer Director allows and encourages directees to feel their blocked negative emotions and safely express them. Once the anger, shame, fear, and sadness is vented, peace, joy, love, and sometimes mystic ecstasy can flood in. The Seer Director listens to directees talk through their hurt, until their relationships are transformed and intimacy is restored. The Seer Director magically transforms directees' negative energy by compassionately taking in their pain and sending back love and healing energy.

Seer Directors are concerned about the directee's total health, and so they encourage exercise and proper nutrition for the body, rigorous thinking for the mind, and honoring one's feelings for emotional health. All of these promote self-esteem and help the directee feel better and become more loving, and therefore more spiritual.

The Seer Director avoids any mind-body dualism. The Seer Director channels the directee's "sky energy" (inspiration, visions, and dreams) and grounds it in the earth (the facts of the directee's everyday existence). They help directees transform reality by joining directees in the search for their spiritual path and vocation, and once these are found, the Seer Director encourages the directee to build a better world. Seeing is about transformation of people, civilization, and the Earth.

The Seer Director may use rituals, or encourage the directee to use rituals, to change the directee's consciousness, to heal, connect with spirit, transmute reality, focus the mind, or change commitments from the old to the new. The Seer Director may use simple rituals of exorcism to help the directee let go of a relationship, bad habit, problem, or psychological attachment. The main overall impact of Seer Directors on directees is liberation and freedom, as they let go and let God more and more.

Seer Directors who are the spiritual directors of groups might use rituals to focus group energy or visualization on healing someone and thus produce a genuine miracle. Seer Directors know how to use ritual to align individuals and groups with the will of God.

As was said earlier, Seer Directors learn to heal others through healing themselves. They practice their own private rituals of prayer, meditation, and centering, which keep them connected with their deeper self and the cosmos. They might use centering rituals, mandalas, labyrinths, mantras, icons, or sacred objects such as crucifixes to unify their consciousness, get rid of internal static, and align their conscious mind with their personal unconscious and the collective unconscious, their body with their emotions, their will with the Higher Power. Before doing spiritual direction, they align all these powers and energies with the work to be done, so that the Great Spirit and healthy cosmic forces flow through them to the directee.

Seer Directors listen to their intuition, whether in the form of an inner voice, feeling, or vision. They are thus aware of hunches that pay off for the directee. They are aware of subtle emotional changes in themselves and in the directee. They see coincidences or synchronicity in directees' lives that has deep significance for them. Highly spiritually developed directors may have paranormal psychic powers such as clairvoyance.

Healthy Seer Directors are aware of, and integrate, their Shadow into their consciousness so that they do not inadvertently use their Seer power for evil purposes. Recognizing their Shadow teaches them humility, so that their healing of others is motivated by caring rather than self-aggrandizement or unconscious forces. Facing the greatest Shadow, that is, their own mortality and death, enables the Seer Director to say "no" to the temptation of short-term ends such as wealth or fame. Death is the constant companion and advisor of the true Seer Director. As someone said, "The wise man and wise woman always walk with the fingers of death tangled in their hair." This allows them to be free, lighthearted, and serious all at the same time.

The Seer Director finds other like-minded directors and forms a peer-supervision group to stay humble, loving, and grounded. The fellowship of their peers heals Seer Directors and makes their path less lonely. They know their place in the cosmos, their interdependence, and need of others. Guided by their peers, their own deepest wisdom, and their Source, Seer Directors claim their power without grandiosity. Their greatest power, naturally, is their ability to link the directee with the power of the divine to save, redeem, and forgive them. The Seer Director is a conduit for God's grace and forgiveness so that people can forgive themselves and others.

Heroic Seer Directors might make their own inner Trickster their other constant companion (besides death), so that they keep their sense of humor and don't take themselves too seriously. The Trickster prevents self-adulation, pomposity, and self-righteousness in the Seer Director. The Trickster is the perfect antidote to self-deception through denial, rationalization, and other defense mechanisms. The Trickster keeps Seer Directors in touch with reality and their own vulnerability.

From Seer Directors a directee learns true humility, to let God be God and let humans be human. Directees become more centered on God, more aware of synchronicity in their lives, more conscious of their Shadow and their own mortality. This in turn causes them to see the wisdom in "storing up treasures in heaven" by committing themselves to eternal values and eschewing what is fleeting and temporal.

THE LOVER DIRECTOR

The goal of the heroic Lover Director is the directee's bliss, oneness, and union with God. The Lover Director also hopes to be in a relationship of God-centered love with the directee, since respectful love between the director and directee facilitates the directee's growth in loving God and receiving God's love. The Lover Director's fear is the directee's loss of love for God. The response of Lover Directors to a problem is to love it, and they teach the directee to do the same, to love and embrace all things, including pain and death. The task of Lover Directors is to follow their bliss, that is, love of God, commitment to God, love of the directee, and commitment to the directee's spiritual well-being. Their gifts to the directee are spiritual commitment, passion, and ecstasy. The Lover Director models all this, and therefore teaches it to the directee.

The Lover Director has a genuine love for the directee, that is, a love that involves staying with the directee through thick and thin, the ups and downs of the directee's spiritual life. The Lover Director is totally committed to the directee, until termination of the relationship seems appropriate. Even after termination, the commitment continues, for the Lover Director is still interested in, and prays for, the directee's spiritual growth.

Lover Directors realize their inability to fully love the directee unconditionally through their own power alone, and so they accept their shortcomings as a Lover and call upon God in prayer to help them love in this way. Only through connecting with the divine can Lover Directors let totally unconditional love flow through them.

When directees feel the unconditional love of God through the Lover Director, they feel new hope, confidence, peace, freedom, and joy arising in them. They realize they no longer have to earn God's love and so now desire to do God's will out of a spirit of gratitude for all God has given them. They no longer operate out of a fear of not being good enough for God.

Lover Directors may experience emotional and sexual attraction to directees, but they contain this within appropriate boundaries. If they fall in love with a directee, wise Lover Directors realize they are projecting their emotional and romantic needs onto the directee and that no human being can satisfy all their longings. Beyond that, they know that the director-directee relationship is a professional one, and although it is all right to fall in love with the directee, to act out their infatuation in any way would involve a serious breach of professional ethics. *Eros*, in terms of sexually acting out, is *not* all right, and so Lover Directors need to clear their feelings for the directee outside of the director-directee relationship with a therapist or another director in peer supervision.

Amor, the total physical, emotional, and spiritual bonding love between a married man and woman, also is obviously not appropriate for the spiritual direction relationship. However, *philia*, or friendly fellowship bonding, and brotherly or sisterly love, are perfectly acceptable between the Lover Director and directee and are to be encouraged.

Agape, the love of God for humanity expressed on the cross, that is, totally unselfish, compassionate, self-giving love of one person for another, which may involve sacrifice of the Lover Director's time, energy, and comfort for the higher cause of the directee's spiritual growth, is also highly appropriate, particularly when the directee is one of the marginalized members of society.

True Lover Directors are willing to do spiritual direction with the poor and homeless free of charge, to do it in hospitals, nursing homes, and prisons, and to give themselves in pure generosity and charity, without expectation of reciprocation of any kind.

Lover Directors have a general appetite for life. They are full of energy, aliveness, and passion. They are fully human and fully alive. They think, imagine, speak, and act with vividness and enthusiasm. As with all the archetypal directors, they teach the directee by example. Their Lover archetype rubs off on the directee. The Lover Director wants to satisfy the directee's longing for creativity, meaning, and well-being. They want to completely know the directee. They instinctively trust the directee, and are willing to be vulnerable with them. They want the directee to be passionately connected to, and in love with, the Earth, nature, work, a cause, a religion, people, and God.

The directee's life thus expands due to the Lover Director. Directees become more involved in their religion, the lives of other people, their work, various causes, and the care of the Earth.

Lover Directors love fun and play of all types. They are far more lighthearted than the other archetypal directors. They encourage directees to be childlike, to live with their senses wide open, to enjoy life, their body, and their sexuality without shame, to revel in the gloriousness and wonders of God's creation. They joke and laugh with the directee and encourage the directee to find God in the playfulness of sports, sex, humor, imagination, relaxation, reading, writing, art, and music. Directees thus rediscover their inner child.

Lover Directors help the directee understand and feel the oneness and interrelatedness of all things and to be empathetically connected to the universal consciousness of God that underlies everything. They promote sensitivity and vulnerability in the directee and also the ability to feel the pain of others as well as their joy. The directee thus opens up more and more to the poor and the marginalized.

Lover Directors help the directee recover from misplaced or disordered love that has resulted in addictions of all kinds:

alcoholism, workaholism, consumerism, addiction to sex or pornography, and so on. They support directees who mourn the lovelessness, lifelessness, and loss of deep feeling in themselves and others. They call directees to give up cynicism, to forgive God, themselves, and others, to embrace suffering and to believe in goodness and grace again.

Healthy Lover Directors are aware that love is a decision more than a feeling, so they commit themselves to *love* the directee, even though they may not *like* the directee. They know that feelings of love for the directee may come and go. So whether or not the feelings are there, they commit themselves to the spiritual well-being of the directee. They forgive directees who do not live up to the Lover Director's image of them. They persist in serving the directee whether or not they are inspired by love. They recognize that, just when their love for the directee seems dead, a new breakthrough of intimacy and intensity may occur. Again, by modeling the nature of true love for the directee, the Lover Director teaches the directee about love without explicitly saying anything. Directees learn the meaning of committed love through the Lover Director.

The Lover Director gifts the directee with an "aesthetic consciousness," the ability to experience all of life as art. The Lover Director has subtle but powerful feelings for everything and helps the directee develop this capacity. Since Lover energy is the source of spirituality and mysticism in all religions, the Lover Director is a natural mystic who can help directees in their search for union with God and in their quest to bring this sense of union into everyday life.

Lover Directors are extremely sensitive to directees and their moods and motives, and this can be painful for the Lover Director. In feeling one with others, the Lover Director cannot avoid feeling their pain. The Lover Director is acquainted with sorrow and grief as well as joy. Following what Paul said, the Lover Director "bears all things" and "endures all things," and helps the directee learn to do the same. Due to the Lover Director's compassion, the directee feels less alone and less abandoned by God. Through the Lover Director, directees know in a concrete way that God is their constant friend and companion.

Following Jesus, Lover Directors will help directees confront and question humanly created religious laws if they feel the laws block true love. They will help directees live in the tension between sensuality and morality, love and duty, passionate experience and responsibility to authentic religious law. They will oppose all legalism in directees, that is, putting law before love. Lover Directors' deep feelings cause them to oppose overly ascetic, overly moralistic, and overly rational religion in directees.

In spite of all the felt tension in their lives, heroic Lover Directors will integrate the opposites and help directees to do so as well. They will affirm the God-given goodness of pleasure and desire and also the God-given goodness of boundaries for conduct, such as the Ten Commandments. They believe in *responsible* sensuality and sexuality that is neither unbridled nor repressed. They use the Warrior's boundaries, the Seer's containment, the Sovereign's order, and the discipline of all three for integration and wholeness. They help directees to do likewise.

Lover Directors use the Sovereign to help directees define limits for themselves so they can channel their feelings in creative directions. Lover Directors assist directees in accessing their Warrior when they need to act decisively, or to cut themselves free from immobilizing sensuality. The Seer in the Lover Director can help directees see the big picture, so they avoid narrow or one-sided love for just their family, nation, or religion to the exclusion of others. Lover Directors expand the directee's world.

The Seer in the Lover Director discerns the directees' boundaries, the Sovereign in the Lover Director helps directees set their boundaries, and the Warrior in the Lover Director assists directees in defending the boundaries, so that people do not easily take advantage of them. The Warrior in the Lover Director teaches directees tough love for the good of all. The Lover Director aids the directee in respecting others' boundaries and in making sure, through the other three archetypes, that the directee's own boundaries are respected.

Lover Directors see each person as a unity of body and soul and believe the body and its natural urges are good, not enemies. To them, sexuality is holy, nurturing, gentle, and loving. They can thus help directees become sexually mature so that they see the inner beauty of women and men and relate to them as a whole person. The Lover Director helps the directee have a committed sexual relationship with one other committed person, and to see this as a way to experience God's love. Through their partner directees learn to receive God's love and to love God in return. The directee learns from the Lover Director that to love and be faithful to your spouse is to love and be faithful to God.

If directees are priests, religious, or anyone else committed to celibacy, the Lover Director can help them discover hundreds of ways to love others without having sexual intercourse. The Lover Director helps directees, whether they are single, married, religious, or priests to remove from their heart selfishness and fear and any other blocks to love. The Lover Director knows how to have intimate friendships, and so helps the directee in this. Directees find that they not only have more friendships, but deeper ones as well.

The Lover Director is understanding, compassionate, and sensitive on sexual matters, so directees feel comfortable sharing this delicate area of their life. Lover Directors have faced their own sexual Shadow and fears. They approach sexuality with gratitude. They find God through pleasure and touch. They know sexuality is a way to God. They image God as the Supreme Lover who enjoys and facilitates every kind of love: between spouses, parents and children, friends, humans and animals, particularly pets. They celebrate the human body and its urges and instincts, and integrate them into their total, holistic self. They help directees do all of the above too.

The Lover Director celebrates with directees when erotic love has brought them closer to God through the ecstasy and joy of healthy physical union with another person in a moral way. They are also there for directees when erotic love brings them sadness, depression, abandonment, and pain, or when their safe, self-sufficient emotional world is shattered and they lose emotional control through the experience of falling in love. The Lover Director helps the directee find God's love in the midst of all this.

The Lover Director also helps directees develop a strong identity so they can contain the intense passion of eros, which often lacks prudence and practicality and takes risks. The Lover Director helps lovers be friends before anything else, so that their passion is built on the holy ground of friendship with each other and with God.

Lover Directors help directees develop a passion for justice. They encourage directees to access their own inner Lover and Warrior, to feel the pain of the poor, and to take decisive action on their behalf. They facilitate the directee's integration of eros and agape, passion and compassion, so that the directee is passionate about ethics and justice and the Earth. They wake the directee up to the suffering of the Earth. They encourage the directee to cherish the Earth, not exploit it.

The power of Lover Directors comes from within, from their inner charisms, their gifts from God, rather than from position or authority in an institution that gives them power over others. The Lover Director's power with directees is the power of love. Directees flock to them because they feel so loved in their presence. The Lover Director respects and does not violate the erotic energy that naturally occurs in mentoring between the powerful and less empowered, for example, between therapist and client, pastor and parishioner, director and directee. For directees who have been sexually abused, it can be profoundly healing to experience being truly loved by a powerful person who never misuses that power.

Lover Directors forgive and accept both themselves and others as a matter of habit, since they know that what they are most critical of in others is a projection of their own Shadow. They also accept infatuation with others for the same reasons. They know that what they adore outside themselves carries the positive Shadow projection of the deep wisdom in their own soul. They lovingly accept all parts of themselves and others, both the negative and positive Shadow, both the potential for evil and the hidden treasure, the inner gold, the good things they and others hide, deny, and repress about themselves. In being aware of the negative Shadow, Lover Directors prevent it from being acted out. They help directees understand all this as well, so that in total self-acceptance directees can be made whole and give birth to their true self.

Lover Directors let themselves be and let themselves feel. They avoid incessant doing, regularly pausing to let their senses take in the richness of the world. They can thus help the directee be grounded in the here and now and appreciate life.

Through the Lover Director, the directee sees the whole world as more vivid, alive, and meaningful. The Lover Director thus brings abundant life to every directee.

The Lover archetype keeps the other archetypes humane and loving and related to each other and to the real world of struggling humans. Without the Lover, the Sovereign Director, Warrior Director, and Seer Director would be essentially detached from life. The Lover gives them their ultimate purpose and keeps them from becoming domineering, sadistic, or manipulative.

The primary belief of Lover Directors is that God, the source of all love, loves them personally and unconditionally. Knowing God's love allows Lover Directors to fall in love with God in an absolute and final way, so that everything in their lives revolves around God's love and is grounded in it. This frees them to love God and others in deep intimacy. Lover Directors are thus not afraid to disclose their own feelings and secrets to the directee, if Lover Directors deem it appropriate, that is, if they discern it will help the directee's spiritual growth. Their lack of fear of being weak and vulnerable serves as a healthy model for the directee. Directees learn that they are totally acceptable to God as they are.

The male Lover Director, unlike many men, is comfortable with being loved by others, being the beloved as well as the lover. The male Lover Director is mature and therefore recognizes, appreciates, and responds to love when it is offered. He does not feel that to receive love is too passive, too feminine. The male Lover Director can both give and receive love. He does not think that, in order to be a man, he has to repress his anima, his inner feminine side. He does not let cultural expectations or societal roles warp the archetypes within him. Since he is in touch with his feminine side, he feels comfortable around women, and understands them. By his example and his expert spiritual direction, he helps the male directee in all of the above as well, so that the male directee feels comfortable giving and receiving love.

The male directee feels free to love a male Lover Director who knows how to graciously receive love. The wonderful experience of males bonding in authentic love, that is, deep male friendship, which is so rare in our society, will cause the male directee to seek out churches, synagogues, and mosques where the male leadership knows how to give and receive love in this way as well.

To sum up, in the presence of a Lover Director, whether male or female, directees feel new desire, new enthusiasm, new life being born within them. They feel the freedom and excitement of being wholly integrated in body, senses, emotions, intellect, and spirit. They feel a new responsibility and care for everyone, particularly for the poor and the Earth and all its creatures. They sense the love and grace of the Spirit pouring through them, others, and the whole creation without measure, and they become mystically united with all.

Chapter Seven

HOW ANTIHEROIC SPIRITUAL GUIDES FORM ANTIHEROIC SEEKERS

In Christian churches, or in any religious organization, just as there are some priests, ministers, and laity who approach the ideal, heroic archetypal model, there are others whose lives revolve around power, guilt, legalism, luxury, or sexual misconduct. Some have replaced service and ministry with politics and social climbing within their institution's structures and are masters of covert manipulation. Others are self-righteous, overly ascetic, rigid, narcissistic, in conflict with everyone, archconservative, jaded, cynical, or burned out. Again, while it may be hard to imagine anyone in ministry being as bad as the antiheroic directors described below, some real-life spiritual guides are not far from the archetypal nadir. In spite of this, there are many reasons why directees do not just quit spiritual direction with antiheroic directors, which I will explain in chapter 9.

The diagram on the next page gives a summary of the four main archetypes of the psyche in their primary, heroic forms as well as the two antiheroic modes associated with each, in relation to the discipline of spiritual direction. The antiheroic forms on the left indicate total possession by the archetype, in other words, all healthy distancing or dissociation from the

**Summary Diagram of the Spiritual Director
as Heroic Sovereign, Warrior, Seer, and Lover
with Two Antiheroic Manifestations Below Each***

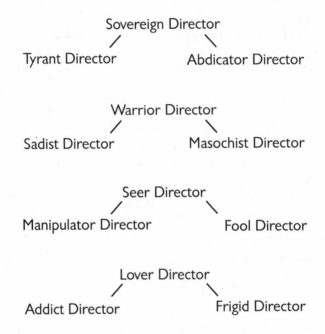

Sovereign Director

Tyrant Director   Abdicator Director

Warrior Director

Sadist Director   Masochist Director

Seer Director

Manipulator Director   Fool Director

Lover Director

Addict Director   Frigid Director

*Adapted from Moore and Gillette, *King, Warrior, Magician, Lover*, 16–17.

archetype is gone. For example, the Tyrant thinks he *is* the Sovereign archetype, rather than its *servant*. On the other hand, the antiheroic forms on the right are characterized by a complete dissociation from the healthy form of the archetype. The ones on the right have none of the heroic characteristics of the archetype. Note: the diagram is not hierarchical; all heroic archetypes are equally important.

THE TYRANT AND ABDICATOR DIRECTOR

The director as Shadow Sovereign is either a Tyrant Director or an Abdicator Director. As a Tyrant the director engages in paranoid attempts to control the director-directee relationship by pretending to be superior to the directee. Tyrant Directors may be priests who have an inflated view of the priestly role, or laypersons who secretly are out for power, which they feel has been denied to them since they have no hierarchical position. The fear of Tyrant Directors is that directees will control the relationship and be in charge of their own lives. Tyrant Directors fear, hate, and envy new life and spiritual growth in directees, which they see as a threat to their sovereignty and feelings of superiority.

Tyrant Directors are not centered in God or the reign of God, and therefore they cannot help the directee be centered in God. Tyrant Directors do not put God the Sovereign in the center of the relationship. They try to usurp God's place as the true Director of the relationship. Rather than having a God-centered and God-directed relationship with the directee, the spiritual direction relationship is director-centered and director-directed. Therefore, the spiritual life of the directee is diminished.

The Tyrant Director does not feel calm and generative in the spiritual direction relationship. Tyrant Directors are insecure and destructive rather than creative. They are suspicious of directees, do not trust them nor believe what directees say about their spiritual experiences. They are resentful of directees who have personal power. They are overcontrolling of the innocent directee who comes to them for help. They destroy the directee's spirit.

The Tyrant Director lacks substance, that is, inner order, authority, and integrity. Although they may not show it externally, Tyrant Directors react with inner fear, rage, and jealousy when directees, mainly by their own surrender to God, reach a new stage of faith development. If the directee is developing an image of God as a compassionate, unconditionally loving

Friend, Tyrant Directors disparage this. Their paranoia that directees might progress beyond them in the spiritual life leads Tyrant Directors to oppress directees by giving them a false image of God as a Tyrant in the sky. If the directee protests against this idol, it feeds the Tyrant Director's paranoia.

Since Tyrant Directors' inflated egos are overidentified with the Sovereign archetype and they want to *be God*, rather than *God's servant*, they constantly need reassurance of their sovereignty, that is, that they are the center of the spiritual direction relationship. They want to be revered and adored by the directee.

Tyrant Directors think nothing of exploiting and abusing the directee. They use the inequality of power in the director-directee relationship to pursue their own self-interests of feeling superior to others, making money, or making a name for themselves as a director. Tyrant Directors charge more than is necessary and want the directee to come back more often than necessary.

Tyrant Directors do not feel the pain of their directees and so are merciless and ruthless. Terrified of their own hidden weakness and lack of potency, they hate and fear all others' strength and talent. They treat all spiritual beauty and joy with cynicism. They kill the spiritual enthusiasm of directees by verbally assaulting and denigrating them. They cause directees to doubt the authenticity of God's presence in their spiritual experiences. The Tyrant Director may even sexually abuse directees of either sex by condemning their sexuality or by inappropriately hugging, touching, fondling, or kissing them when they are most vulnerable.

Tyrant Directors are jealous, enraged, or anxious if the directee expresses any interest in switching to another director.

They find the directee's praise of other directors, clergy, therapists, or workshop or retreat leaders intolerable and very threatening to their own ego. Tyrant Directors try to persuade the directee that these other people are really inferior or incompetent in comparison with them, and the directee should have nothing to do with these competitors for the directee's affection.

Although Tyrant Directors are not centered, they believe they are the center of the universe and that directees exist to serve them by bringing them their money, praise, and even their souls to do with what they like. Their narcissism seeks to be worshiped by directees. Tyrant Directors' delusions of grandeur cause them not to be concerned with being a good and just steward of God's realm; their only concern is themselves and their own superiority, fame, power, and financial benefit.

Tyrant Directors are overly sensitive to criticism by directees. Unless they feel totally in control, Tyrant Directors will not do periodic reviews with the directee of the spiritual direction sessions and the directee's progress (or lack thereof), because the directee may give them negative feedback. Tyrant Directors are not interested in the directee's progress in and of itself. They are interested in the directee's progress only if they think it will boost their own reputation and get them more clients. If the directee criticizes them, they may fly into a rage or quietly smolder. Though the reaction of Tyrant Directors to criticism may appear threatening to the directee, Tyrant Directors really feel weak and deflated. They mask their sense of worthlessness and vulnerability with anger.

Behind the Tyrant Director is another Shadow Sovereign, the Abdicator Director, who either abdicates all responsibility for the spiritual direction relationship, or makes up for lack of spiritual power by overcompensating, that is, overidentifying

with the Sovereign archetype and becoming the Tyrant Director. In the case where Abdicator Directors feel they are nothing
if not identified with the Sovereign energy, they tend to project
their own weakness, which they hate, onto others, and then
attack them in order to prove to themselves that they are powerful. Since they perceive the other person as weak, they believe
they will be victorious. Since they reject their own weakness,
they reject it in others. They like to humiliate, criticize, and
abuse those directees whom they perceive as weak in spiritual
discipline, rigor, and asceticism.

Abdicator Directors who have become Tyrants cannot stand
it if they give the directee advice, or even a command, which
Abdicator/Tyrants like to do, and the directee fails to obey them.
Lacking inner security, the Abdicator/Tyrant Director is tormented by fears of disloyalty from their directees, either fearing
directees will not do what they tell them to do, or worse yet,
they will "go over to the other side," that is, find a better director. Abdicator/Tyrants are defensive, hostile, and cruel with
directees and use shady tactics to dominate them. Their central
concern is domination and control.

As Abdicator/Tyrant Directors become more and more domineering and dictatorial and arrogate more and more power
to themselves, their paranoia about losing power and control
grows, and so all inner orderliness, peace, and calm is destroyed
in them and their directees.

On the other hand, Abdicator Directors may totally disidentify their ego with the Sovereign archetype, and feel de-
prived of any access to it. In this case, they feel starved of
Sovereign energy and power, and the true Abdicator Director
emerges. Abdicator Directors then project the Sovereign energy
they are not in touch with onto the directees and become dependent upon them. They see the directee as being in control of the

director-directee relationship and themselves as impotent and incapable of acting or feeling calm and stable when with the directee. They ascribe more power to directees than they actually have. Directees, on their part, may see themselves as dependent on the director, and so their relationship becomes codependent.

The *abdication of power* syndrome of the Abdicator Director can be just as disastrous for the directee as the *usurpation of power* syndrome of the Tyrant or Abdicator/Tyrant Director. Abdicator Directors refuse to let the transformative power of the Sovereign God flow through them to the directee. They refuse to lead the directee away from sin and toward goodness. They refuse to be committed to the directee or to take any responsibility for the directee's well-being. They avoid all authority, even when God wants to speak through them with authority (not authoritarianism, which comes from the Tyrant Director). For example, out of fear that directees may not like them, Abdicator Directors fail to warn their directees about the possible perilous consequences of adultery or stealing from their employers.

Abdicator Directors never mentor anyone or generate any life beyond their own narrow narcissism. They never stand firm on spiritual principles and values, but just tell directees whatever they want to hear. They want to please directees out of a misguided desire to be popular. When directees ask them to clarify a difficult church teaching or hard saying of Christ, Abdicator Directors refuse to say anything they think may be unpopular and tell directees to do whatever feels good to them. Abdicator Directors avoid or ignore objective truth. They may be nice, sensitive, and gentle, but they do not convey to directees any of God's substance, gravity, and authority. Eventually directees lose respect for Abdicator Directors since they are too wishy-washy and never challenge directees. Directees then bring about the Abdicator Director's self-fulfilling fear by quitting spiritual direction.

Neither the Abdicator Director nor the Tyrant Director listens to or serves God, or the people of God. Both speak untruth. Tyrant Directors say whatever serves themselves. The Abdicator Director says whatever the directee wants to hear. Neither say things that serve the building up of God's reign.

Tyrant Directors need to achieve power over others to possess any sense of self-worth. They compensate for their emotional insecurity and psychological impotency by grasping at power and authority. They operate by intimidation, force, guilt, shame, manipulation, pettiness, and narcissism. If Tyrant Directors are depressed or elated, theirs is the only mood that counts. Directees have to adapt to the Tyrant Director's mood, cater to it, and sacrifice their own mood to it.

Tyrant Directors try to ensure that no one under their direction really flourishes and breaks free of their spiritual chains. And if directees do become liberated, the Tyrant Director takes all the credit for it. Tyrant Directors try to keep directees imprisoned, dependent, not able to solve their own spiritual problems and move on in the spiritual life, because otherwise directees might feel that the initial concern they brought to spiritual direction had been resolved, and so quit.

Tyrant Directors banish creativity on the directee's part. Their selfishness, narrow-mindedness, vindictiveness, and lack of imagination means Tyrant Directors may throw a self-righteous tantrum if directees try something new on their own. Tyrant Directors are prone to either indolence and self-indulgence, or Spartan rigidity and intolerance. Everything they do, or refuse to do, is for personal aggrandizement. In the spiritual direction relationship, Tyrant Directors lack balance between their needs and the needs of the directee. They always put their own needs first. For example, the directee always has to accommodate the Tyrant Director's appointment schedule. The Tyrant Director has no sense of negotiation or flexibility with the directee.

The arrogance of Tyrant Directors cuts them off from divine wisdom. They do not consider themselves accountable to God or anyone. They believe they are a law unto themselves and their spiritual direction ministry is their own irrevocable realm, not a gift from God. They have no sense of being called to serve others. They are not interested in the poor and powerless or injustice. They want only rich directees as their clients. They would never consider doing spiritual direction for free in a jail or psychiatric hospital or in a community center in a slum. Thus, Tyrant Directors are cut off from their own humanity. They have a scarcity mentality. They are not in touch with the overflowing abundance of God's grace, and therefore the spiritual gains of others must be their own loss.

The Tyrant Director sucks energy out of directees by employing shame and putdowns, by offering no support and no affection, and by being sarcastic and cold. Tyrant Directors are rigid, one-sided, and inflexible; they demand unquestioning obedience and are authoritarian and condescending. They encourage directees to maintain the status quo in their lives, even when the status quo is unfair. They never relate to directees as peers and individuals in their own right. They dismiss independent thinking by the directee.

Tyrant Directors are legalistic in their theology. They find faults in directees and never see them as "good enough." They are interested in church law and order, not grace. They emphasize the Ten Commandments over the Beatitudes. They are not interested in underlying attitudes and values, but in what "thou shalt not do." Dissent by the directee is considered to be disloyalty. Since the spiritual direction relationship is based on domination, there is only pseudointimacy between the Tyrant Director and directee.

Tyrant Directors believe that their own authoritarianism reflects God's authority. Both male and female Tyrant Directors project their own patriarchal view onto God and the church. Their God is the Cosmic Judge, just waiting to punish wrongdoers and send them to hell for eternity. They believe that God is only male. They believe that God ordained patriarchy. They take the image of God the Father literally rather than metaphorically.

When Tyrant Directors are tempted, they choose evil: the misuse of the power imbalance of the director-directee relationship for ego aggrandizement. They secretly feel empty, but they cover up this feeling by deriving pleasure from dominating others.

The directee feels fearful, confused, and disempowered by the Tyrant or Abdicator Director. Directees feel unsure of the validity of their spiritual experiences. They feel cursed rather than blessed, discredited rather than affirmed, and discouraged rather than enthusiastic. They feel either intimidated and threatened by God, if working with a Tyrant Director, or they feel cut off from God's transformative power and love, if working with an Abdicator Director.

Under the Tyrant Director directees become scrupulous and legalistic, and under the Abdicator Director they feel God is absent and just does not care about what they do. The Tyrant's and Abdicator's misuse of power causes directees to feel cynical. Rather than pursuing their spiritual dreams of union with God and their spiritual aspirations of creating a just realm, they become afraid to trust God and themselves. Their life becomes more hellish than heavenly. The directee, in short, has become more antiheroic than heroic.

A subtheme of this book has been the idea that lack of male leaders operating out of the heroic archetypes has resulted in lack of participation by men in religious functions. The male Tyrant Director curses younger male directees rather than blessing them. The male Tyrant Director's guidance of young men establishes disorder in their lives by modeling dishonesty and corruption.

Young men feel abused by the male Tyrant Director and cannot develop their own heroic inner Sovereign Director so that they can spiritually guide their own life. Male Tyrant Directors undermine the masculinity of their male directees. They don't want them to access their own Warrior or Sovereign energy because then the male directee might really grow spiritually, or leave them, or at least control the director-directee relationship.

The male Tyrant Director makes the male directee into a victim, someone who blames and shames others for the directee's own lack of spiritual growth. The male directee may criticize injustice but never do anything about it, while at the same time claiming innocence and moral superiority. Under Tyrant Directors, directees become passive-aggressive in their spiritual growth: wronged but self-righteous.

The male Abdicator Director, on the other hand, causes young men who are seeking authoritative (not authoritarian) guidance to lose respect for God and God's church, synagogue, or mosque. Male Abdicator Directors who have lost their own connection to God, who are not competent spiritual directors because they have only dabbled in spiritual direction, who are unrecovered alcoholics, who have abdicated the throne by being physically present but mentally absent in the spiritual direction sessions, or who are depressed rather than joyful, cause male directees to feel contempt for spirituality. And if the director is a sexually aggressive Tyrant, or a sexually impotent Abdicator who is racked with unhealthy sexual guilt, it prevents young men from integrating sexuality and spirituality in a healthy and responsible way. If young men find their priest or minister to be a Tyrant or Abdicator, they will flee the church.

The Sadist and Masochist Director

The director as a Shadow Warrior is either a Sadist Director or a Masochist Director.

The Sadist Director turns the Warrior Director's detachment from human relationships into cruelty. The Sadist Director can be cruel with or without passion. When Sadist Directors are under a lot of stress they can have a passion for destroying the directee's spiritual life. Sadist Directors may belong to extremist right-wing religious groups that are very frightened and angry about changes in their religious tradition. They may feel that their self-concept as true believers is threatened by liberal-thinking or New Age directees. Rather than trying to understand directees and why they believe what they believe, Sadist Directors objectify them as spiritual enemies, enemies of their so-called orthodox faith, and ascribe evil motives to the directees. Sadist Directors use this objectification to justify their nonnegotiation and nondialogue with the enemy. The Sadist Director puts down and humiliates any directee with a different spirituality, particularly one based on trust and God's grace.

Sadist Directors, convinced without a doubt that they have all the truth, will use any means to defeat the enemy, killing their spirituality with no sense of remorse for the loss of faith development. They cannot tolerate doubt, questioning, or speculation on the part of the directee. Sadist Directors presume

their own religious and moral superiority, their own righteousness, and are usually blind to their own dirty battle tactics, such
as self-righteous judgment, anger, and the lovelessness of their
own ways. Like the pro-life fanatic who shoots and kills abortion doctors, Sadist Directors have little or no awareness of their
own sin.

Sadist Directors' goals and plans are cynical and self-serving:
to convert the directee to the Sadist Director's own narrow spirituality. Sadist Directors therefore divide the world into two
camps in an egocentric way: people who oppose their approach,
whose spirituality must be destroyed, and people who are weak
and give in to their approach, who must be indoctrinated further
into it.

Sadist Directors are the foundation for the formation of cults,
in which participants in the cult totally give their minds and
wills to the cult leaders, even to the point of committing suicide, as happened in Jonestown. The victims of cults have to do
whatever the leader says, no matter how painful or degrading.
Asking questions is considered heretical or sacrilegious. The
cult leaders are totally convinced of their own rightness and are
totally oblivious to the pain they are causing their followers.

In spiritual direction, the effect of a Sadist Director on the
directee is that the directee feels intimidated, violated, and confused. Directees may have felt liberated by their faith up to this
point, but now they feel bound, and that it is not acceptable
to think for themselves and follow their own conscience. They
may now feel that there is only one way to look at things and
that asking questions shows a lack of faith rather than being a
means to a deeper faith. They may be shocked by the aggressive-
ness of the Sadist Director, and wonder, if they are Christians,
if being judgmental and angry is an acceptable part of being a

follower of Christ. Or they may just leave the church and their new-found faith behind.

Sadist Directors are not interested in any kind of spirituality of social justice. They have no real concern for the weak, poor, or vulnerable in our midst. They love to defend and spread spiritual patriarchy, that is, churches, synagogues, and mosques controlled by antiheroic and immature men. They love to lay heavy burdens on others without lifting a finger to help them.

The *boy psychology* of the male Sadist Director makes him particularly interested in destroying, or at least repressing, the inner Warrior of women. Sadist Directors consider women to be spiritually subordinate and morally inferior.

Male or female Sadist Directors battle against the power of the feminine within themselves. They hate everything soft and relational. Feminist spirituality is anathema to them. Their fear of being swallowed by the feminine within leads to spiritual brutality, not only against women but against men as well. They try to convert their directees to extreme self-discipline, legalism, asceticism, and scrupulosity, that is, obsessive guilt about inadequate performance of minute details of ritual trivia.

The spirituality of Sadist Directors is one of perfectionism rather than of accepting their imperfections and need of God. They believe in human perfectibility and works-righteousness. In other words, they believe that God will accept them into heaven once they are perfect. They always have their spiritual sword out, see spiritual dragons and Satan everywhere, and believe the only options are fight, flight, or be destroyed. They are continually embattled and perceive everything as a spiritual slight, threat, or challenge to be confronted. They are usually very uncomfortable with *the flesh* (the body and sexuality) and *the world* (secular society) and may withdraw into a monastery (the flight response), or at least adopt a holier-than-thou attitude.

Directees under such directors feel their worldview progressively more narrow. They become filled with anxiety and guilt about whether or not they are doing everything perfectly. As with the Tyrant Director, directees start to see God as the Cosmic Judge, Bad Cop, or Shadow Warrior. They become rigidly obsessed with details, like the Pharisees who Jesus accused of multiplying so many minute, man-made religious laws that they strained out gnats and swallowed camels, tithing herbs but ignoring the weightier matters of the Law such as justice, mercy, and faithfulness.

Like Tyrant Directors, Sadist Directors are in it for their own personal gain, in whatever form that takes. They are soldiers of fortune and behave like mercenaries. They use Warrior skills for their own benefit. They can either be totally unconcerned with ethics, or so totally concerned with ethics that they become legalistic and self-righteous in a way that harms the well-being of the directee. For example, Sadist Directors may be overly zealous about social justice to the point that, out of anger at transnational corporations, they encourage directees to protest with physical violence as a way of getting revenge. Sadist Directors use directees as a means to their own personal ends rather than valuing directees as an end in themselves.

Sadist Directors have enormous self-discipline, but they are overly rigorous because they are driven by their own compulsions and fear. They have no humane feelings or higher ideals or values. They sacrifice principles to money, status, and power. They are obsessed with winning, that is, getting their own way, and competing with other directors for directees. They strive to have more directees than the other directors in their area, as if spiritual direction was a contest.

Like the Tyrant Director, Sadist Directors fight to be in control of the spiritual direction relationship and to keep directees dependent on them. Also like the Tyrant Director, their ego, not God the Holy Warrior, is at the center of their spiritual direction practice. They advise directees in ways that get them even more tangled up in sin. For example, they advise directees to just seek their own advantage in secular affairs, without regard for others, causing chaos in the community and business world. In spiritual affairs, they may advise a person to find a more intensely spiritual spouse, even though they know this will cause a marriage and family to break up. Sadist Directors know that Charismatic and Pentecostal Christians in particular are susceptible to this temptation and often do leave their spouse because he or she is not as "spiritual" as they are.

The directee learns to put aside ethics, ideals, and principles and to compete ruthlessly in the world. Anyone who is poor or weak or less spiritually enlightened, including one's spouse, is considered a hindrance and cast aside. The directee has no sense of social responsibility and thus acts unjustly. The resulting pain may rebound and eventually destroy the directee.

Sadist Directors, since they are not inwardly secure, measure themselves by their performance in the outer world. Their deep anxiety and low self-worth may generate a compulsive personality disorder and they may become workaholics, seeing one directee after another, keeping them coming back every week rather than the standard once a month. Sadist Directors ignore their own pain and burnout and that of their directees.

Sadist Directors spend the spiritual direction sessions verbally attacking everything and everyone, trying to prove that their worldview or their theology is the only right one. Directees are forced either to give in, to fight back, or to quit. Directees may find themselves fighting with the director about issues, such as homosexuality or abortion, that they had never formerly given much thought to and that have nothing to do with why they came for spiritual direction in the first place. The spiritual direction sessions revolve around the Sadist Director's issues rather than those of the directee.

Sadist Directors are always crusading for a cause — their cause. They are never a Lover who just enjoys life. They have no healthy Sovereign or Seer in them to help them see things more broadly or in perspective. Initially they work incessantly to "save" others, that is, convert them to their point of view, but eventually they burn themselves out and end up treating directees even more callously and cynically.

Like the Tyrant Director and Abdicator Director, the Sadist Director and Masochist Director are closely linked. Sadist Directors harm both themselves and directees who cannot live up to their impossible standards. Sadist Directors feel that both themselves and their directees are never good enough, never spiritual enough, and so mercilessly abuse themselves and others. They don't take care of their mental and physical well-being. They do not know when to terminate an unhealthy spiritual direction relationship. Sadist Directors obsessed with "success" try to repress the Masochist within but get caught in self-punishing behavior, forging ahead no matter what the danger signs, working eighty hours a week, until they have a heart attack or their family deserts them.

The Masochist Director is the passive pole of the Warrior Director's Shadow and lies just beneath the Sadist Director's rage. Masochist Directors project Warrior energy onto directees and experience themselves as powerless. They do not defend themselves psychologically; they let directees criticize them unjustly, push them around, and exceed the limits of their self-respect and psychological and physical health. They are *too* service-oriented and have no boundaries. They see directees whenever directees want, without consideration for their own needs. For example, they let directees call them at home and at all hours of the day and night.

The Masochist Director may be extremely liberal, and may therefore be easily intimidated by strongly opinionated, judgmental, or conservative directees who are convinced they are right about everything. Masochist Directors let the opinions and moods of directees totally dominate the spiritual direction session, without challenging or confronting them.

Like Abdicator Directors, Masochist Directors stand for nothing. If they do have some definite beliefs, they do not stand up for them. Although they believe in social justice, they will let right-wing directees berate the poor, without opposing them. They let their personal values be trampled on. They let directees violate their personal space, disparage their beliefs, call them names (such as "commie" or "fag lover"), and even shout at them. They feel anger, shame, unworthiness, inadequacy and confusion, but do not fight back. They feel paralyzed and believe themselves to be victims, which leaves their souls open for more invasion.

Masochist Directors lack vigor and are depressed and cowardly. They lack the capacity to endure the pain necessary to fight against the aggressive directee. They instead duck issues, avoid direct confrontation, and feel defeated. Lacking energy, resolve, and determination, they do not know how to say no to their directees. They are in bondage to their directees, and their lack of ego-strength makes their life unbalanced, resulting in loss of self-respect, and possibly their health. They may take abuse for too long, until they explode with verbal or even physical violence against directees, screaming at them or throwing them out of their office.

Up until that point, directees working with a Masochist Director may get the impression that there is no authority in the religious tradition, that everything is wishy-washy, that they can believe whatever they want, that no one is there to put boundaries on, and oppose, either their liberal or conservative views. The result is confusion and moving away from the truth and a well-balanced sense of reality. Directees working with a Masochist Director learn to violate other people's spiritual and physical boundaries.

Sadist Directors see directees as a threat to their narrow values, react to directees with rage, and, possessed by the Warrior archetype, try to poison or damage directees in any way possible. Masochist Directors, on the other hand, are too accommodating and nice, too comforting, coddling, and soothing, and never take any risks that might be unpopular with directees. Whereas the Sadist Director confronts directees too much, the Masochist Director confronts them too little. Totally dispossessed of the Warrior archetype, Masochist Directors believe in peace at all costs, even if it involves repressing bravery and their true values and beliefs.

Whereas Sadist Directors try to force their values and beliefs on directees, Masochist Directors allow directees to be in control and impose their beliefs upon the director. Whereas Sadist Directors don't care if directees hate them, Masochist Directors sacrifice their true selves in order to be liked, which usually leads to what Masochist Directors fear, that is, the directee's contempt for them.

In neither case is the antiheroic Warrior Director concerned about truth and justice, what God's will is, or what is best for the directee. Sometimes people need tough love from their spiritual director if they are to grow spiritually. They cannot be allowed to dodge painful issues forever. On the other hand, they also need to be treated in a respectful way and not violated. The true Warrior Director speaks the truth with love.

Like the Shadow poles of the Sovereign Director, the Shadow poles of the Warrior Director do not allow God to be the center and director of the spiritual direction relationship. In the case of the Tyrant Director and Sadist Director, the director is the false center and director. With the Abdicator Director and Masochist Director, the directee is the false center and director. In none of these cases can the directee spiritually grow, nor can the reign of God be promoted, developed, and brought forward.

Directees working with a Sadist or Masochist Director feel bound, anxious, guilty, narrowed, and intimidated in the one case. In the other they become overly bold, presumptuous, and unjust and do not learn appropriate boundaries or their place in the order of things. For everyone involved, in both cases, there is disorder, God's will is not done, and directees again become more antiheroic than heroic.

The Manipulator and Fool Director

The Shadow Seer Director, either in the form of the Manipulator Director or the Fool Director, does not apply the Seer's gifts with compassion.

Manipulator Directors use their specialized training to their own advantage. Being obsessed with spiritual power, they lust after it. They play on the directee's fears, misrepresent the facts, and distort the truth in order to deceive the naive or innocent directee. They manipulate the codependent nature of the needy and vulnerable, their difficulty in saying no to someone in authority, and their need for consolation and support. Manipulator Directors violate trust and take advantage of directees' weaknesses for their own goals and gain.

Manipulator Directors keep directees dependent upon them and use them for monetary, sexual, or political purposes. Like Tyrant Directors, they overcharge for their services and have directees come for unnecessary visits. They maneuver directees by withholding key information. When they share information or knowledge, it is usually just intended to impress directees with their learning and superiority. They do not guide and initiate directees by degrees that they can handle and integrate into their lives. Like Sadist Directors, Manipulator Directors have become so detached from people that they are cruel.

Directees feel fearful, confused about the truth, unfulfilled, and codependent. They may feel "underwhelmed" by not being given what they need, or overwhelmed by being insensitively initiated into things too rapidly so that they do not have enough time to process them.

Manipulator Directors can be secretive on the one hand and, on the other, engage in outright lying, laying claim to wisdom and knowledge they do not really possess. They may, for example, claim to be an expert in Ignatian or Carmelite spirituality, which they really know little about. Then they attempt to cover up their ignorance in a web of rhetoric that says nothing, even though it sounds learned.

Manipulator Directors are clever, but not wise. In spite of all their knowledge, they are fools. They take delight in humiliating their directees for their ignorance, or get so caught up in ideas or theories that they lose sight of the reality of the human situation. Trying to be superior by using their knowledge to belittle and manipulate directees, they become inferior.

In hurting directees, Manipulator Directors hurt themselves. Their cynical detachment from genuine human values cuts them off not only from their directees, but also from their own souls. In withholding their hearts from others and not sharing others' joy and pleasure, Manipulator Directors wind up isolated and lonely.

Directees feel baffled by the Manipulator Director's rhetoric. They feel put down and ignorant in the presence of the Manipulator Director. Directees feel that they have nothing to offer, no wisdom of their own, and that they need the Manipulator Director's wisdom, and yet Manipulator Directors are so detached and inaccessible that directees feel they cannot connect with them and get what they need.

The Manipulator Director who is highly educated manipulates directees in a subtle intellectual way beyond just disparaging the directee's beliefs. Manipulator Directors may overemphasize reason to the exclusion of intuition, feeling, and imagination. They may allow analysis and rationality to dominate to the point of closing themselves and directees off from the unconscious, from hunches, dreams, emotions, the nonrational, and the mysterious. They may be unfeeling judges of the directee's more charismatic spirituality. They may come across as cold, heartless, dogmatic, aloof, and pompous, evaluating the spiritual experiences of others as unworthy of consideration.

On the other hand, Manipulator Directors may emphasize intuition and feeling to the total exclusion of rationality and analysis. They may manipulate directees by discouraging them from being critical and using their own God-given intellect. The Manipulator Director can then talk with impunity about the Tarot, I Ching, astrology, runes, kabbala, angels, animal medicine cards, and so on. These may or may not have some truth and merit, but in the hands of the Manipulator Director they become tools for manipulating gullible directees. The Manipulator Director can spout any kind of New Age psychobabble about these things with absolutely no accountability.

Intellectually oriented Manipulator Directors judge the spirituality or theology of their directees as "not good enough" or judge their spiritual methods as "not doing it right." They are not interested in what the spirituality or spiritual practice or methods of directees does for them. What Manipulator Directors want is for directees to see and do things *their* way, that is, what Manipulator Directors consider the *proper* way. They are more interested in converting directees to their way of thinking and their way of spiritual practice than in converting them to God. In spite of all their knowledge, Manipulator Directors may have a very narrow view of God and how God works in the world.

Under the Manipulator Director, directees come to believe that their own spiritual experiences are worthless, invalid, and faulty. They start to feel doubtful and disconnected from their own soul and gut, from their deepest intuitions and instincts. They sense that their image of God is narrowing and they start to feel disconnected from God. They find themselves living more and more in their head rather than their heart. Alternatively, with a New Age Manipulator Director they may feel cut off from their critical faculties and too much into intuition and fantasy. They may feel confused and unable to ask any hard questions because they are expected to just accept whatever the director says.

Intellectual Manipulator Directors cannot see directees for what they are because their worldview gets in the way. Manipulator Directors have an inflated view of their own theories and knowledge and take criticism of their ideas as a personal attack.

They manipulate life intellectually rather than living it. They think and observe and analyze life but never live it, and so their religious experience is limited. They become sterile voyeurs of their directees' lives. By their example they teach their directees to be disengaged from life, and even to fear life.

Manipulator Directors name people and their religious experiences in ways that diminish them, for example, calling a religious experience "unorthodox" or "neurotic" or "magic." They thus diminish directees' self-esteem and their trust in the authority of their own experience. They may make the directee spiritually or even emotionally or physically ill by passing negative judgments. They lessen directees' possibilities and hopes for the future. By rigidly labeling people and their experience, they dehumanize them.

Having fallen prey to arrogant egoism, Manipulator Directors live their lives in service to pain, ruin, and hatred. They use their power to harm, not heal. They are secretly delighted by their directee's misfortune. They teach the directee to use imagination negatively. By constantly asking, "But if you do that, what if such-and-such happens?" they cause the directee to imagine negative things happening, which then become self-fulfilling.

The Manipulator Director is caught in the grip of the Seer's power Shadow. On the other hand, those out of touch with the Seer get caught in the passive pole of the Seer's Shadow and become Fool Directors. Fool Directors want the spiritual status and power of the Seer Director, but not the responsibility. Whereas Manipulator Directors get power by seeking it in a fairly overt and sometimes obvious way, Fool Directors get power (at least in their own mind) much more covertly, by destroying the power of others or by depriving them of power. They do not want to help others like true Seer Directors, in a careful, step-by-step way, nor become skilled at channeling power.

Fool Directors are envious of those who live fully. They deflate others in order to give themselves a sense of importance and to cover their own desolation and lifelessness. Like Abdicator Directors, Fool Directors take no responsibility for the well-being of the directee. They commit sins of both commission and omission with directees, but hide their hostile motives behind feigned naiveté. They are slippery and elusive and hard to confront. If challenged, the Fool Director acts bewildered and questions the intuition of directees that something is wrong in how they have been treated. Fool Directors make directees who confront them ashamed of their suspicion. The directee senses covert manipulation behind the Fool Director's smokescreen of innocence, but the directee cannot describe it. Directees always feel undermined, but they cannot put their finger on what is happening.

Fool Directors are enmeshed in their own emotions and problems, to the point of experiencing inner chaos. Unable to act effectively themselves, they are passive-aggressive but claim innocence when accused of any ill intentions. They love to subtly derail those who are making worthwhile efforts, while denying their own hidden power motives. They consider themselves too good to try or take risks, but they block others who do and seek their downfall.

Fool Directors may bury themselves in various addictions to escape self-knowledge. They do not want to go on the inner journey, learn from their mistakes, get in touch with their feelings, or suffer the pain of inner transformation. Just as they avoid developing the true self of directees, so they avoid their own true self.

The Shadow Seer Director, whether as Manipulator or Fool, is a kind of Shadow Trickster. They both use humor, not to lighten things up, but as a weapon to put directees down, through subtle sarcasm and derision. Whereas the heroic Trickster tries to reveal the truth through playing tricks or telling stories or parables, Fool Directors try to hide the truth to maintain their covert games. And while the Trickster aims at the necessary task of deflating our grandiosity, the Manipulator and Fool Directors work at deflating us and inflating themselves.

Without authentic humility and love, the antiheroic Seer Director can do great harm. Possessed by the Seer archetype, Manipulator Directors see themselves as the source rather than the instrument of Deep Wisdom, the Wisdom of God, and so their inflated egos come between the directee and God. Dispossessed of the archetype, the Fool Director, out of envy, prevents the directee from being empowered by God.

Since God does not tolerate spiritual arrogance and sin, antiheroic Seer Directors, whether as Manipulators or Fools, sooner or later get caught in the spider web of their own lies and deceit, are publicly exposed, and come to ruin. There are many proverbs in the wisdom literature of all major religions about how sin eventually finds the evildoer out. Just to take some Jewish examples: "the way of the wicked leads them astray" (Prov 12:26) or "the faithless are ruined by their duplicity" (Prov 11:3).

The directees of the Manipulator and Fool Directors feel completely befuddled and yet unable to articulate what is wrong. They feel demeaned, undercut, doubtful, and foolish. Whereas before they were full of life and enthusiastic about sharing their religious experiences, now they are shut down and unsure. They feel codependent, unfulfilled, despairing, and in desolation. In short, they have become antiheroic.

The Addict and Frigid Director

The Shadow poles of the Lover Director are the Addict Director and Frigid Director. The Addict Director's main question is, "Why should I put any limits on the pleasure I get out of religion, out of doing spiritual direction, and out of my directees?" The main characteristic of Addict Directors is spiritual lostness, that is, they have no spiritual boundaries. Their egos are inflated to the point where they think they are God, and the directees are there to serve their pleasure.

The Addict Director is a religion addict, a kind of spiritual glutton or spiritual consumer who cannot get enough of religion and piety. Addict Directors spend all their time meditating and praying, reading scripture and spiritual books, and going to church. But they never actually help anyone, even in their spiritual direction sessions.

Addict Directors are awash with spiritual consolation, bliss, and ecstasy, and never want to come down to ordinary, non-ecstatic living. Their spiritual practices and love of rituals interfere with their job (if they have a job other than being a spiritual director) or with their responsibilities to their family or religious community. They spend all their spare time in religious workshops, courses, and retreats. They disregard the requirements of the legitimate authorities in their lives: bishops, religious superiors, congregations, or spouses, because Addict Directors claim their only commitment is to God, which in fact is just a subtle disguise for total commitment to the desires of their own egos.

Addict Directors are off-center, out of control, and never satisfied because they are trying, under their own power, to stuff "the hole in their soul," that is, there is some spiritual pain, wound, or emptiness that they are trying to assuage or fill up with religion. Their ego and its needs are at the center, not God. Their ego cannot let go and let God be in charge of their life, which may require them to sometimes do difficult things.

Therefore, Addict Directors are not *indifferent* to whatever happens to them. (Ignatius of Loyola recommended that we all strive for *holy indifference,* that is, the willingness to let God have God's way with us, whatever that is. We should not care what God wants us to do, as long as we know we are doing God's will.) Addict Directors are only willing to give in to God's will if they perceive it as being in line with their own desires. In other words, their ego wants to remain fully in control.

Addict Directors always have to be on a spiritual high. Even when they are doing spiritual direction, Addict Directors are not primarily interested in helping people. Their primary interest is to revel in the spiritual consolation they experience as they listen to directees describe their spiritual experiences. Spiritual direction for the Addict Director is an experience of vicarious spiritual thrills. Addict Directors are pseudomystics who are not willing to go through the dark night of the senses, or the dark night of the soul, either their own dark nights or those of directees.

Addict Directors may be nature mystics, getting joy and ecstasy from indulging their senses in the colors and beauty, sights, sounds, and smells of the world, but they may not be open to contemplating the ugliness and injustice of life. Their spirituality is an escape from the harsh realities of life. Their spirituality is flighty, soaring blithely above the world and the problems in people's lives, rather than being grounded in reality, which is grounded in God. At best, the Addict Director has only a surface experience of God.

The great danger for the directee is that the Addict Director may encourage the directee to become a religion addict as well. The Addict Director may encourage the directee to engage in unlimited prayer, meditation, church-going, or involvement with church activities. The Addict Director may praise directees for being involved in the Nineteenth Annotation, the Charismatics, Cursillo, the Twelve Steps, and the Secular Franciscans all at the same time, as well as encouraging directees to spend two or three hours a day praying, reading scripture, saying the Rosary, and spending all their spare time (if they have any!) looking at spiritual Web sites on the Internet or watching religious television programs. Meanwhile, directees are often late for work or uninterested in it, and their spouses feel neglected and are thinking of leaving them and trying to find someone who is interested in them and the children.

Addict Directors are victims of their own sensitivity, but they have to learn, often the hard way, that spiritual boundaries, that is, moral rules, ethics, discipline, and restraints are useful. Otherwise, they end up having affairs with their directees or authority problems with bishops, superiors, or other church leaders, or spend too much of their family's finances on spiritual books and workshops, and encourage directees to do the same.

Directees may at first be in awe of the Addict Director's religiosity and feel they need to do much more themselves, particularly when the Addict Director encourages this. At first this greater involvement in church and prayer may seem fulfilling. However, when more and more involvement is prescribed, without limit, the directee starts to feel bound rather than liberated, compulsive rather than free, burned out rather than renewed. The directee may also feel a great sense of guilt at wanting to cut back, as well as a sense of lostness and hopelessness that can lead to depression. As Ignatius said, evil spirits often come to us as angels of light, tempting us with good things that, if taken too far, become evil. Evil spirits can also come to us in the guise of a spiritual director or guide!

Addict Directors find God through the pleasures of food, good living, and sex, which is healthy enough, but they are tempted to do it to excess, without respect for themselves or others or the dictates of God against luxury, lust, adultery, or gluttony. For many spiritual directors, it would be easy to separate sexuality from genuine love, step across the boundary, and become sexually promiscuous, particularly with directees who are physically attractive or in great need of affection in their lives.

Addict Directors are unable to commit themselves to directees who are in long-term desolation or who are suffering either physically or emotionally. Addict Directors tend to be fickle with directees, keeping only those who bring them the most pleasure. When there is conflict the Addict Director feels uncomfortable and changes the subject or refuses to keep seeing the directee. Thus, Addict Directors remain on the surface of the director-directee relationship. They never walk with the directee to the bottom of the directee's issues, the Valley of the Shadow of Death, as the Bible puts it, and therefore little spiritual growth occurs.

Addict Directors are fickle with their relationships outside of spiritual direction as well and therefore have few enduring friendships, resulting in a sense of loneliness and isolation. This drives them to seek satisfaction for their need for love through their directees. They may become infatuated and fall in love with one of them, whether male or female, and become addicted to this directee, or at least obsessively fixated on him or her. Therefore, they feel destroyed when a directee "leaves" them, that is, stops coming for spiritual direction.

Addict Directors are jealous or envious of others in the directee's life. They may become possessive of the directee if the directee shows any interest in becoming involved with a therapist or a different director. They may subtly try to undermine the directee's relationship with anyone else who has a claim on the directee's love, even that of close friends, relatives, or spouses. If directees are having difficulty in their marriage, the Addict Director may encourage them to leave their spouse, when the problem could easily be remedied with counseling. The Addict Director may even be a "siren" and try to lure directees from their spiritual quest, calling, or vocation if it necessitates that directees move away from the director to take more training.

If the Addict Director oversteps the sexual boundaries of the director-directee relationship, the directee will feel shocked and profoundly violated. If the Addict Director avoids suffering and conflict in the directee's life, or drops the directee when things get intense or difficult, the directee will feel profoundly bewildered or abandoned. If the Addict Director tries to lure directees away from other relationships or from their spiritual quest, directees will have a deep sense of unease.

The absorption of Addict Directors in their feelings and in sensory perceptions from directees (such as perfume, eye color, hair color, or body curves) blocks the directors' ability to really listen, direct their own thoughts, and be in control of themselves in the directee's presence. They may be so caught up in the pleasure of the moment that they cannot remember things the directee said in previous sessions, or even five minutes ago. Addict Directors may be intoxicated by being with the directee and focused on the swirl of their own myriad sensual impressions, rather than being grounded in the oneness of God, which could bring them calm and stability. They may be unable to step back, detach, and gain distance from their feelings, from their lustful desires, or from a destructive, addictive relationship with a directee.

Addict Directors are eternally restless in the director-directee relationship, never able to settle down and seriously tackle one spiritual area of the directee's life. In an insatiable hunger for excitement, adventure, or some new spiritual experience, they ask the directee too many questions, or skip from one topic to another, unable to focus on one spiritual experience at a time. They compulsively extend the frontiers of their own spiritual experiences no matter what the cost to themselves or the directee. They love to recall and talk about their own spiritual experiences in the spiritual direction sessions, rather than focusing on directees and their experiences.

Directees may feel that they are directing the Addict Director rather than the other way around. The directee may also feel frustrated with the Addict Director's inability to be detached and objective with what the directee brings to the session. Frustration for the directee may result as well from skimming across the surface of issues, so that nothing substantial ever seems to get done.

Heroic Lover Directors are bound not by external rules, but by their own inner structures and by their rootedness and centeredness in God. Addict Directors are caught in idolatry: they make relative, fragmentary spiritual experiences their Absolute. They do not see the whole world with its good and evil, justice and injustice. They escape from the whole by focusing on the part that brings them pleasure. In spiritual direction they do not focus on the whole person, but only on the good, light, and pleasurable parts of the directee's experience. With a woman, a male Addict Director may just focus on parts of her anatomy rather than seeing her as a whole person, a unity of body and mind, heart and soul, virtue and sin, light and dark. Therefore, he cannot have a full, genuine director-directee relationship with her.

Addict Directors caught in idolatry are inflated. They unconsciously identify themselves with God, the Supreme Lover. They restlessly search for a "fix" that will ultimately satisfy them, but only God can do that. Dissatisfaction with their own limits and the limits of their directees keeps them searching for a continuous high. At the same time, they lack boundaries, which are what they need most, for boundaries can give them appropriate distance and detachment from their directees. Addict Directors need to own their own humanness, their human limits. They need to discover that they are not God. They can then call upon and surrender to God's help.

Addict Directors need the heroic Sovereign Director to define limits for them, to give them structure, to order their chaos. They need the heroic Warrior Director to use the sword of the Spirit to cut them off from all their worldly attachments. They need the heroic Seer Director to help them detach from their emotions, to reflect and become objective, and to see the whole, the big picture, not just the parts.

In dealing with Addict Directors who have not been reined in and balanced by the other archetypes, directees will feel enmeshed with the director, and also fragmented by the Addict Director's idolatry, that is, the director's focus on individual, fleeting religious experiences rather than being rooted and grounded in God.

Addict Directors are possessed by the Lover archetype. Frigid Directors, on the other hand, are completely detached from the Lover. The life of Frigid Directors seems sterile to them and to the directee. They have flat affect, a lack of enthusiasm for the spiritual direction work. They take no joy in the spiritual direction sessions or in directees. In the midst of a session Frigid

Directors feel bored and listless, speak in a monotone, and constantly check the clock. They feel alienated from the directee, that the spiritual direction session is not worth doing, or they feel bored that the session is going nowhere. They can't wait for the session to end. Everything, including spiritual direction, is vanity, that is, useless.

Frigid Directors feel chronically depressed and unable to connect emotionally with directees. They also cannot connect with their own emotions. Their failure to bond with directees leaves Frigid Directors unable to commit themselves to directees and their spiritual growth. Like Addict Directors, they have no interest, ability, or energy for doing deep work with directees, to walk through spiritual deserts with them.

There can be dozens of reasons why Frigid Directors are emotionally disconnected. Frigid Directors may not know how to get close or be so wounded that they cannot get close. They may come from a family or culture that is extremely emotionally reserved. They may be afraid of losing themselves or their identity, being dominated by the directee, or failing at spiritual direction. They may be afraid of falling in love with the directee. They may fear losing their vocation of being a single man or woman, of being a religious sister or brother or priest. They may fear losing their celibacy because they equate celibacy with superior holiness. They may be dominated by feelings of shame or guilt, a lack of self-worth, or feelings of being unlovable. They may fear being abandoned by directees who stop coming, or think, "What's the point of doing spiritual direction? Directees just come and go. You get attached to them and then they leave."

Frigid Directors may believe that they need to be an authority figure to the directee and therefore cannot display any sign of weakness or vulnerability, such as communicating love for the directee. They may be established in a dual relationship with the directee: they may also be the directee's leader or teacher and therefore feel that they cannot be the directee's friend. It may be a long-term spiritual direction relationship, and they may be bored by the directee constantly repeating the same issues.

Whatever the reason for the Frigid Director's emotional disconnection, the directee will learn by example also to be emotionally disconnected from God and others. Directees will feel drained by the spiritual direction session, like the life and energy have been sucked out of them, as if the Frigid Director is a psychic vampire, a soul-sucker, or a spiritual black hole. The directee will absorb the Frigid Director's shame, guilt, low self-esteem, boredom, listlessness, and rigidity and come to associate all this with religion.

The male Frigid Director may be patriarchal, lack any divine image of the feminine, and thus disassociate feelings from God. Many males have been taught since boyhood that they should not be afraid or sad, and that feelings are shameful. Therefore, they cannot access their sadness, anger, joy, or love. They believe feelings are immature or narcissistic, or that feelings may lead to dependence and vulnerability, which are inappropriate for a man. They have been taught that men should always be in control, dominant, competitive, and emotionally invulnerable. Or the male Frigid Director may be overly rational and intellectual and distrust feeling and intuition. He may live in the ivory tower of his head.

The male Frigid Director may not have gotten over early training that sexuality is sinful, selfish, and degrading. Therefore, he represses any sexual feeling. Repression of eros may lead him to publicly rail against lust, while subconsciously being possessed by it, or secretly addicted to pornography. The male

Frigid Director may be physically impotent, or he may see himself as a machine and women directees as prey. He may use sex with directees for physical release or to satisfy his lust for power and dominance over women, whom he considers inferior. He may dehumanize and objectify directees so that he can use them as objects. He may feel that bodies are unclean and may be alienated from his own body, which he may abuse. He may project his repressed eroticism onto women and believe all female directees are promiscuous. He may believe he has to give up or repress eros to reach agape, which he considers the only acceptable spiritual form of love.

The unhealthy sexuality of the male Frigid Director will make female directees feel degraded, uncomfortable, and disillusioned, particularly if he inappropriately crosses their sexual boundaries. Male directees will be turned off by the lack of warmth from the male Frigid Director and his inability to bond emotionally in a healthy way with other men. Male directees also will be turned off by the hypocrisy of male religious or priests who have been called to celibacy and who disobey God by getting sexually involved with women or other men. The solution to the lack of male involvement in religious affairs may be more heroic male role models.

Male or female Frigid Directors, disconnected from their feelings, have no real motivation to do spiritual direction. At best, they might feel that they are living in an emotional fog. At worst, they feel unreal or dead inside, cut off from their heart and soul. Or they may only experience negative emotions: boredom, anger, stress, depression, fear, or anxiety. In any case, they are emotionally impotent. They feel no joy, aliveness, or healthy passion about anything. If they have been wounded by directees who have stopped coming, to protect themselves from more pain they may numb out their inner Lover, or create boundaries so strong that they become a rigid shell preventing any emotion from getting in or out. In feeling no compassion or love, the Frigid Director is similar to the Sadist and the Manipulator Director.

In every case, whether the antiheroic director is a Tyrant, a Masochist, a Fool, an Addict, or any of the other Shadow archetypes, either the director or directee has become the true focus of attention. God is not the center of the director-directee relationship and therefore cannot bring about the spiritual growth of the directee.

With the Addict Director, directees feel bound, compulsive, enmeshed, guilty, lost, fragmented, and violated. With the Frigid Director they feel isolated, abandoned, frustrated, listless, drained, and disillusioned. In either case, the antiheroic director has again succeeded in forming antiheroic directees.

Chapter Eight

BECOMING A HEROIC
GUIDE OR SEEKER

If spiritual directors or guides and spiritual directees or seekers want to operate out of the heroic archetypes, the first thing to do is to identify which of the archetypes is most active in their lives. There are a number of steps they can take to do this.

The first step is to ponder the positive attributes of the Sovereign, Warrior, Seer, and Lover archetypes and the negative attributes of the Tyrant, Abdicator, Sadist, Masochist, Manipulator, Fool, Addict, and Frigid given in the summary of key characteristics below. The second step is to study the positive and negative actions of the spiritual director who operates in a heroic or antiheroic way described in chapters 6 and 7. Both directors and directees can then simply ask themselves, "Which archetype do I think is dominant in my life?" They can also ask, "What would others who know me well say about this? Would they say that I tend to be a heroic Sovereign, antiheroic Manipulator, or what?"

THE HEROIC ARCHETYPES:
KEY CHARACTERISTICS

Sovereign: responsibility, service, stability, largesse, magnanimity, nobility, order, holding the center, creativity, blessing, justice, protection, security, prosperity, benevolent power, authoritativeness, realism.

Warrior: courage, discipline, self-control, alertness, strategy, tactics, willingness to suffer, adaptability, assertiveness, loyalty, emotional detachment, decisiveness, endurance, single-mindedness.

Seer: right-brain/left-brain balance, intuition, secret knowledge, wisdom, healing, ritual, initiation, alignment with the cosmos/God, reflectiveness, thoughtfulness, rationality, integration of Shadow and opposites, channeling of energy and divine grace, transformation.

Lover: passion, ecstasy, enthusiasm, generosity, romance, forgiveness, sensuality, sexuality, aliveness, vividness, connection, play, enjoyment, seeking oneness, sensitivity, vulnerability, embracing pain, creativity, gratitude, compassion.

THE ANTIHEROIC ARCHETYPES: KEY CHARACTERISTICS

Tyrant: fearfulness, uncenteredness, death-dealing, disorder, suspicion, self-aggrandizement, arrogance, injustice, ruthlessness, intimidation, demanding adoration/worship, overcontrol, authoritarianism, suppression of others, malevolent power.

Abdicator: irresponsibility, powerlessness, torment, defensiveness, dependence or codependence, hostility, stinginess, pitifulness, silence, woundedness, oversensitivity, overgentleness, masking weakness with rage or humiliation of others.

Sadist: cruelty, violence, objectification of others, mercilessness, constant embattlement, loves of destruction and others' pain and torture, absence of ethics or ideals, willingness to compromise any principle in order to "win."

Masochist: defeat, low pain tolerance, cowardliness, overaccommodation of others, absence of vigor and determination, lack of psychological or physical boundaries, absence of integrity, passivity, avoidance of confrontation, absence of defenses.

Manipulator: lust for spiritual power, distortion of truth, withholding of information, manipulation, lying, violation of trust, greed, cynical detachment, exaggerated rationality, overemphasis on left-brain or right-brain, cold, head-knowledge, excessive intuition, use of New Age psychobabble to mislead.

Fool: dishonesty, denial of involvement, envy, hidden hostile motives, passive-aggressiveness, feigned naiveté, slipperiness, elusiveness, covert destructiveness, sarcasm, grandiosity, ego-inflation.

Addict: enmeshment, unbounded sensuality, gluttony, lostness, insatiability, chaos, fickleness, lack of discipline, narcissism, seductiveness, restlessness, fragmentation, jealousness, infatuation.

Frigid: lack of commitment, lack of enthusiasm and imagination, repression, isolation, sterility, flat affect, numbness, boredom, listlessness, puritanism, disconnection, loneliness, depression.

BECOMING A MORE HEROIC
SPIRITUAL GUIDE OR SEEKER

With the above lists of characteristics in mind, spiritual directors or directees could be more conscious of archetypal characteristics displaying themselves in their daily thinking, conversations, and actions.

- Do they think in terms of blessing and affirming others, confronting them, manipulating them?
- Are they decisive, aloof, or compassionate in their behavior?
- Is their speech competitive or wise?

They could also reflect on their favorite characters and saints in the religious literature of their tradition: the Hebrew Scriptures, New Testament, Koran, the Hindu and Buddhist canon, and other spiritual writings and poetry. They also could ponder their images of their earthly father and mother, and their images of God:

- Do they identify with Esther, Solomon, Elijah, Mohammed, Rumi, Kabir, Ramakrishna, Vivekananda, Buddha, Buddhaghosa, Lao Tzu, Joan of Arc, Jerome, the Virgin Mary, Mary Magdalene?
- Which of the four heroic and eight antiheroic archetypes have they seen in their mother or father?
- Is God a heroic or antiheroic Sovereign, Warrior, Seer, or Lover to them?

How they see their father and mother, and how they see God, may tell them a lot about which archetypes are operating within them, because we tend to project our inner consciousness outside ourselves.

In midlife there arise opportunities to integrate archetypes that are undeveloped or underdeveloped in our psyches because, as we have less energy to suppress them as we get older, they begin to call for attention. For wholeness and full union with God, we must befriend our Shadow archetypes.

The Shadow archetypes are not evil in themselves, but they have a propensity to cause us to engage in evil actions when we don't pay attention to them. They may emerge in unexpected and uncontrolled ways. When we are aware of them, we can control them.

Spiritual directors or directees can ask God to free them from any areas of unfreedom, faults, or compulsions. For example, directors or directees may have an excessive need to be in control, to be thanked or appreciated, or to win or get their way, or they may have an excessive fear of intimacy or rejection. Thus, the Tyrant, Sadist, Manipulator, or Frigid may be affecting them. If they are continually repressed rather than acknowledged and integrated into our psyche, negative archetypes just become stronger and more dangerous. Prayer is our greatest asset in achieving needed integration. Through the grace of God, we receive the courage to face and integrate our Shadow.

Exposure of one's Shadow side is naturally resisted. The Shadow is, by definition, what we want to hide, deny, and repress about ourselves. So working with our Shadow can be extremely difficult, and we may need outside professional help from a trained depth psychologist. However, spiritual directors or directees could also, after identifying what they think is their main archetype, choose a patron saint for themselves who they think most clearly exemplifies the positive side of that archetype, and then pray to that patron saint to help them be on the redeemed side of the archetype and to deal with the Shadow side in a healthy way.

As any Catholic knows, it is not the case that saints have any power in and of themselves to effect change. However, once saints are asked for help through our prayers to them, they can petition God with our requests. Just as anyone, whether Catholic, Protestant, Muslim, or Jew, might ask a particularly holy friend to pray for them, so saints are believed to have special influence with God. God listens to everyone, but God may give particular attention to those who have done the most, or suffered the most, for God's reign. This is part of what the "communion of saints" means: we ask our brothers and sisters who have gone before us into heaven to help us.

The first step of directors or directees should be to admit and accept their powerlessness over their Shadow when they try to deal with it on their own, in other words, to admit they need the help of someone outside themselves. In fact, the Shadow can be integrated into our lives in a healthy way only by the grace of God. We are the branches and God is the vine, and we can do nothing constructive without God.

Part of being heroic is keeping an appropriate tension between our main archetype and the other three heroic archetypes, so that they balance each other out. For example, a good religious leader (Sovereign) keeps a healthy tension with the wise man or woman (Seer) and prophet (Warrior) and also maintains a contemplative prayer life (Lover). Spiritual directors or directees might study and pray to a balancing archetypal figure. For example, if they have too much of John the Baptist (the spiritual Warrior) in them, they might pray to David (the spiritual Lover) to make them more like the shepherd boy who composed and sang songs of love to God.

Another method would be for the spiritual director or directee to use positive personal affirmations, for example, "By the grace of God I am a heroic Warrior. I cut through deception and subterfuge and decisively go to the heart of the matter. I battle others' demons with them and persevere with them no matter what the odds, until we are victorious!"

Jung believed that pathology does not lie in the existence of Shadow archetypes within us but in consciousness no longer being able to control the unconscious. When that happens, a need arises in the self for the integration of the unconscious into consciousness. In other words, with our true self overseeing things, we let the Shadow into our awareness a little at a time. The only alternatives are to keep repressing the Shadow, and so kill off a vital part of ourselves, or let it flood into our consciousness all at once and overwhelm us.

As we slowly let the Shadow into our awareness, we can make conscious, rational, and ethical choices about what to do about it, and thus we disempower the covert power of the Shadow. Ignatius of Loyola said that evil spirits like it when we keep everything secret. The ManKind Project, on the other hand, says that "secrets kill." We should strive to not keep secrets from others, or from ourselves. In short, spiritual directors and directees need to be engaged in an ongoing inner dialogue with both the positive and negative archetypes within them.

Robert Moore and Douglas Gillette in *King, Warrior, Magician, Lover* outline a number of techniques for becoming a healthier man that could also apply to becoming a healthier woman: analysis of archetypes in dreams, psychotherapy, spiritual disciplines of various forms, meditation on the positive aspects of an archetype, prayer, ritual processes with a spiritual elder or crone, and so on.

However, Moore and Gillette's overarching technique consists of two points: critical self-appraisal and humility.[1] Critical self-appraisal consists in realistically and honestly looking at how the Shadow archetypes are manifesting themselves in our lives. Second, humility also consists of two points: knowing our limitations and getting the help we need, both of which are often hard to do in our culture, since we are supposed to be superhuman, self-sufficient, and totally independent.

The archetypes within us can be developed so that we realize the desired balance of them in our lives. Our true self is like the chair of an inner board meeting, and the archetypes within us are the board members. Each board member needs to be heard from (even the dumb, unpopular, or disgruntled ones), so that the whole person can be involved in the decisions of our lives.

ACCESSING AND ACTIVATING THE ARCHETYPES

According to Moore and Gillette,[2] the following are four ways in which we can connect with the mature archetypal energies within us:

1. *Active Imagination Dialogue.* Like Paul, we often do "the things we do not want to do," due to Shadow archetypes. Active imagination dialogue allows us to contact these negative energy forms by personifying them within us, that is, addressing them as a person, giving our point of view, and listening for their reply. This often works best on paper, writing the thoughts and feelings of both sides without censorship, accepting whatever answers come, either startling or reassuring. To deal with a vicious inner critic in the form of a Tyrant or Sadist, it might be helpful to work with a therapist or to invoke a positive archetypal energy form before starting to write.

"Often, conducting a dialogue with inner 'opponents' — usually forms of the immature energies — will defuse much of their power. What they — like all children — really want is to be noticed, honored, and taken seriously."[3] Once we notice them, they no longer feel compelled to disrupt our lives in order to get our attention. Honoring these energies can bring new balance to us and fulfill ignored aspects of our personality.

2. *Invocation.* Just as active imagination dialogue is a conscious way of talking to yourself, a second technique for

accessing the archetypes as positive energy forms is a conscious way of calling up mental images you want to see, instead of the usual mental clutter. Focused invocation involves first of all finding an image, painting, or sculpture of a Sovereign, Warrior, Seer, or Lover that speaks to your heart or soul. Place the image (for example, a Greek Orthodox icon) before you (or imagine it or get close to it if it is, say, a statue in a cathedral or park). Relax, clear your mind, and converse with the image.

If the image is a Sovereign, this should activate your inner Sovereign archetype. Seek to merge your mind with the Sovereign archetype that comes up within you, while at the same time realizing that you are not the archetype, but the archetype's servant. Feel the power and strength of the Sovereign and the Sovereign's benevolent protection of you. Ask the Sovereign for the Sovereign's authority, blessing, and orderliness.

A final step might be to honor the image of the archetype by burning candles or incense before it. Invocation is basically a form of prayer. Icons and religious sculptures or statues are not idols but ways of focusing the archetypal energy form that is being invoked. *It is not that the archetypes have power in and of themselves, but God works through them to bring God's energy, power, wisdom, and love to us. If God touched us directly, it might overwhelm us.*

3. *Admiration.* Quite simply, younger people need older people whom they can admire and look up to. They can do this by studying their lives either in person, or through books, articles, or audiovisuals. Where the Shadow dominates our psyche, we need to draw upon the strengths of heroic persons through actively admiring them. If we need the courage of the heroic Warrior in our lives, we could study Winston Churchill or Joan of Arc. If we need the wisdom of the heroic Sovereign, we

could learn from Abraham Lincoln, or Canadian Prime Minister Pierre Elliot Trudeau and his attempt to construct the "Just Society."

4. *Act "As If."* In this fourth technique we act *as if* we are already the one we want to be. Emotion tends to follow motion, so if we act as if we are a heroic Sovereign, we will soon start to feel like one. If we need more Lover, Warrior, or Seer, we could act like we have lots of love to give, take decisive actions, or act wise by listening more.

QUESTIONS FOR THE ASPIRING SOVEREIGN, WARRIOR, SEER, AND LOVER

Those who want to become Sovereign Directors or Sovereign Directees can practice being more responsible, noble, service-oriented, magnanimous, benevolent, and just. They can also ask themselves the following questions:

- What Sovereign qualities did my father or mother or other mentors have?

- In what ways were they good or false Sovereigns?

- In what ways am I like them?

- What characteristics of the good Sovereign do I need to access more fully?

- How have I mentored and blessed others?

People who want to be heroic Warrior Directors or Warrior Directees could meditate on and start to develop the following positive characteristics: assertive alertness, passion for justice, integrity, just anger, a willingness to suffer to reach their goals, compassion for the weak, humility (so they can learn from their mistakes), a positive outlook on life, discipline, and so on. They can also ask themselves:

- Who have been the good Sovereigns and just causes I have served?

- What part of the Warrior do I need to access?

- What aspects of my behavior do I need to let go of or cut off?

- What aspects of the Sadist or the Masochist do I see in my father, mother, or myself: unintegrated anger, cruelty, settling disputes by violence (in word or deed), lack of compassion for the weak, inability to say no, letting others run my life, no boundaries or defenses?

- What energizes me when I feel powerless?

- What positive Warrior models have I had? What do I admire about them? How can I access these traits for myself?

Those who want to be Seer Directors or Seer Directees can enhance their Seer power by slowing down in daily life, simplifying their lives, and reconnecting with the deeper, eternal order underlying the phenomenal world — the cosmic Way or *Tao* (the Taoist name for God; similarly Christians call Christ *the Way*) — an order inherent in all of nature and beyond human control. They can be fully aware of all the subtle ways God works in their lives and of where they are serving others.

Aspiring Seer Directors or Seer Directees also can ask themselves:

- Do I use my expertise to serve others as well as make a living?

- Do I overcharge for my services?

- In what ways am I a Manipulator or Fool?

- Do I pretend to know more than I do?

- Do I avoid making others feel foolish for having a certain religious experience, asking certain religious questions, or approaching religion in general differently than I do?

- Do I value intuition as a real form of knowledge?

- Do I pursue inner work, the inward journey?

- Do I have a spiritual director and a faith community myself to whom I am spiritually accountable?

- How well do I wear the mantle of the Seer?

Those who want to be heroic Lover Directors or Lover Directees and who are currently dominated by the Addict should try to practice moderation, discipline, and healthy asceticism and should meditate on the necessity of setting boundaries, so that sensuality does not overwhelm them. Frigid Directors or Frigid Directees could ask the Spirit to fill them with the fire of love, a surge of Lover energy that would enlarge their heart so it is big enough to receive the greatness of God's love and hold in their heart all those who God holds dear — which is everyone!

Aspiring Lover Directors and Lover Directees could also reflect on:

- How did my parents' affection affect my own?

- How do I feel about my body?

- Am I in touch with my feelings and senses?

- How can I be more vulnerable with loved ones?

- How do I see God in others?

- How does my passion for life manifest itself?

- How compassionate am I with others' pain?

OTHER WAYS OF
ACTIVATING THE ARCHETYPES

Pushing down archetypes that would like to express themselves means that directors or directees will feel them initially in their negative forms, which may make them repress the negative archetypes further. Both the inner and outer world of directors and directees may then seem very frightening. If they feel awful, they may be stuck in an archetype in its negative guise. To feel empowered once again, they need simply to examine what archetype has possessed them or dispossessed them and then honor it by expressing it in its positive form. When they learn to integrate the positive side of the archetype within themselves, their inner enemies will be transformed into allies, and they will have a new sense of life and freedom.

To awaken the archetypes within them, all directors or directees have to do is shine the light of consciousness upon them. If they are already active in their negative form, certain symptoms (such as moodiness or being judgmental or impatient) will alert them to this. Again, consciousness will turn the dark archetype to light.

Political buildings (city hall, parliament, congress) are temples to the Sovereign, athletic stadiums are temples to the Warrior, universities and hospitals are temples to the Seer, and churches, mosques, and synagogues are temples to the Lover. Another way for directors or directees to activate these archetypes is to visit these modern-day temples to the four heroic archetypes and observe the people there. They could observe positive and negative examples of each of the archetypes displayed: the Tyrant politician going on a rant, the Sadist athlete out to maim the competition, Seer doctors using all their skills to cure patients, the Lover churchgoer humbly working with the poor in a soup kitchen. They could ask the citizens, amateur athletes, students, and disciples what the characteristics and tactics were of the leaders in these temples who exemplified the best and worst qualities of the respective archetypes, and then study these leaders' lives.[4]

Another way for directors or directees to activate an archetype is to literally ask it to come into their lives and to meditate and journal on how, when, and where it is expressing itself in their lives: at work, home, with friends, in dreams or fantasies. They can also ask who in their lives exemplifies the archetypes in both their negative and positive forms and what they can learn from them.

Directors and directees also can use their imagination to picture themselves acting as a Sovereign, Warrior, Seer, or Lover, and note what feelings this stirs up in them. For example, they could imagine themselves as the Sovereign of all aspects of their lives: they are totally in charge and so can change anything they want. They can ask themselves: What would I decree in my home and work? What new laws would I write? How would I explain the changes and new policies to my subjects? How would I convince other Sovereigns (bosses or spouses) of the wisdom of the changes, so they will cooperate? After thoroughly imagining all this, they can then ask where or how this archetype could realistically be expressed more in their life.

Still another way to identify the dominant archetypes in the lives of directors or directees is for them to write out their life story and compare its themes with themes from archetypal stories. Carol Pearson in *Awakening the Heroes Within* gives an excellent synopsis of archetypes and their stories. For example, the Warrior goes on a journey, confronts and slays a dragon, and rescues a victim. Lovers yearn to love, find love, are separated from their love, and (in tragedy) die or (in comedy) are reunited with their beloved. Sovereigns are wounded and their realm becomes a wasteland; Sovereigns take responsibility for the realm and their own woundedness, and the realm is restored to fertility, harmony, and peace. Seers overcome debilitating illnesses; through healing and transforming themselves, they learn to heal and transform others, as well as to align their will with that of the divine.

If the life-script of directors or directees was given to them by their parents and they now find it too confining or unsuited to who they really are, they can write a new script and find new archetypes for their lives by asking: Who has inspired me? Has it been people who embody the Sovereign, the Warrior, the Seer, or the Lover? What brings me real pleasure and satisfaction? What am I good at? What do I love to do? What would my obituary say if I lived my life to the fullest and on my deathbed had no regrets? What archetypes have been active in my life, and what new ones would have to be active for me to fulfill my potential?[5]

Sometimes people's avocation or hobby is their real vocation. Sometimes an archetype is taking over their life and they are so focused on their present life-script that they don't recognize it. For example, they may have taken over the family business and be running it as a Sovereign (manager), but their real love is playing the guitar because their real archetype is the Lover. Our true archetypes may be found in our dreams, fantasies, daydreams, or what we like to do "on the side" or where our mind goes when we let it wander. No life will make us happy if it is not our own, and no life will make us miserable if we are true to our archetypal story. Therefore, we should follow our bliss, not other people's expectations for our life.

Every director should try to activate the Lover archetype since loving the directees is the most important thing the director does. Developing the Lover archetype gives God a direct channel for expressing God's love to the directee. "The tragedy of failing to develop the Lover archetype far outweighs the collected gravity of the inevitable mistakes one makes in animating it."[6] Directors can first of all activate the Lover by loving themselves, as Christ commands all of us to do: "Love your neighbor as yourself." If directors do not first learn to love themselves, they will not believe that God loves them, and no love will flow through them to directees.

For the Christian, a second main way to develop the Lover archetype is for the director to constantly study the life of Jesus in the gospels, since he is the supreme Lover and all the heroic archetypes are activated in him.

"Putting on Christ" does not mean taking off one's humanity, because Christ is the fulfillment of humanity, the goal of mature humanness. One interpretation of what Christ meant when he repeatedly called himself the "Son of Man" is: "I am the human one." The fully human one is the one who has fully activated all four of the heroic archetypes, since the archetypes are the deepest and best parts of our psyches or souls. The four archetypes are the spiritual heroes within each human being.

God is often portrayed as a Divine Warrior. The God of the Judeo-Christian scriptures is a Warrior who hates battle, yet whose righteousness will not shrink from forcefully confronting the perversion of God's creation by our sins. Liberal churches repress or ignore passages about God and Jesus as Warrior (for example, Mark 13, Matt 24, Luke 21, and especially Rev 19–20), whereas conservative churches take them too literally, as if God was a Sadist longing to destroy the whole world. God as

Warrior approaches us with a sword not to kill us but to cut us loose from our attachments to what passes away so that we can attach ourselves to the Eternal One. By the wounds of Christ, the Warrior for justice (Rev 19:11), we are healed.

Throughout the scriptures the Divine Warrior fights corruption, from the Flood, where God symbolically wipes out all but the righteous Noah and his family, to the liberation of the poor, enslaved, and oppressed Hebrews from Egypt, where, because Pharaoh is so hard of heart, all Egyptian firstborn die and Pharaoh's charioteers are drowned. Yahweh is a true Sovereign and Warrior, a dreadful enemy of unjust Tyrants.

According to liberation theology, God fights with fierce righteousness for justice. The oppressed in the developing world embrace God as Divine Warrior, and the oppressors in the developed world repress or deny this dimension of God. In any case, directors or directees should know that there is a biblical basis for them also to be Warriors who fight injustice wherever they find it in their own or others' lives.

It is also all right for the director or directee to be a Sovereign. The most ancient Jewish, Christian, and Muslim religious texts proclaim that God or Allah is Sovereign over the chaos that all of us experience, and therefore our lives are not random or meaningless. The Sovereign is the archetype of order, authority, and generativity. God as Sovereign rules the world with fairness and justice. God makes the world safe and unshakeable. God is greater than any evil spirit. Christ's main proclamation was the reign of God, and his main invitation was to trust God's sovereignty over our lives. So again there is a solid biblical precedent for directors or directees to be heroic Sovereigns who model their sovereignty after God's, serving the people of God rather than lording it over them.

Since all individuals have each archetype in them in various stages of suppression or development, and since all are forced by life to activate some of each archetype, it can be hard to identify which one is most central for them as spiritual directors or directees. Besides studying the archetypes in depth, they can ask themselves which activities, attitudes, and characteristics associated with the various archetypes would give them the most joy and satisfaction? Which would make them feel most comfortable? If they had free time, which archetype would they act like? Which archetype best explains their life and choices? What would drain or frustrate or feel most foreign to them? Which would be their least preferred way to spend their time and energy? They also could ask others what they think the director's or directee's answer to these questions would be.

Many people find their identity in one archetype and their fulfillment in another. One archetype is dominant and an auxiliary one adds stability, responsibility, warmth, or correction to it, balances it, broadens it, and thus fulfills it. For example, Warrior Directors might develop the Lover archetype so they can better empathize with the pain directees feel. Although difficult for the director, since it involves developing apparently opposite attitudes, values, and priorities, it would have the advantage of helping the Warrior Director be sensitive to being *too* assertive or confrontational. Seer Directors might add the Sovereign archetype so that they are more grounded in reality.

The second archetype may emerge only at midlife when as directors or directees we no longer find energy and satisfaction in our primary archetype. Maturity as a director or directee is about integrating opposites within ourselves, which is the major task of the second half of life. In the first half of life, we are convinced that our personal standpoint is eternally valid and fail to recognize the legitimacy of the other archetypes. Our major archetype determines what we consider to be the right ideals and principles of behavior.

However, as we get older, if we do not start to integrate at least one other archetype into our conscious psyche, we may find that our main archetype is accompanied by disorientation, stress, anxiety, resentment, boredom, and envy. We will start to feel fragmented and as if we are playing a role, which can lead to burnout. So, for example, a woman who has been primarily a Lover in the first half of life may need to learn to be a Warrior in the second half and succeed in the competitive world of business so that she feels she has accomplished something besides raising children.

Spiritual directors can be more in touch with their inner reactions and archetypes through a number of processes, for example: individual or group supervision; asking themselves after each spiritual direction session: what were my feelings? fears? hopes? struggles? joys? needs?; consistently working through their own issues and resistances; praying before, during, and after sessions; asking for the gift of sensitivity, self-awareness, and openness; and being in individual spiritual direction (and counseling as necessary) themselves.

Mature, well-balanced spiritual directors, who have developed each of the four archetypes in themselves as much as they are able, will feel calm and centered, will speak from inner authority based on their own spiritual experiences, and will bless their directees, recognizing them for the full persons they are and having a sense of creating a more just world through them. Heroic spiritual directors care deeply and genuinely for their directees and know the truth of the central commandment of life, "You shall love the Lord your God with all your heart, mind, soul, and strength, and you shall love your neighbor (directee) as yourself."

Men, Archetypal Leadership, and Religious Participation

A subtheme of this book has been a concern that far fewer men participate in religious functions than women. It was noted early in the book that male attendance at any Christian religious function is about 20 percent. This is a problem for all churches, and for the world, if significant numbers of men are not living the gospel.

It is safe to predict that if all religious leaders were heroic archetypal role models of the sort described in this book, that is, true Sovereigns, Warriors, Seers, and Lovers, men would flock to the churches. Real human beings are always a mixture of light and darkness. Therefore, while it will not be possible for most religious leaders to be *totally* heroic, if they were *substantially more heroic than antiheroic,* significant numbers of men would return to the church.

In many ways, male pastors from every Christian denomination are in a dual archetypal role. Their role as religious leader means they are potentially both Sovereign and Seer. The diminished or absent role of the mature and wise father in so many households today means that longing for masculine Sovereign and Seer energy is intense among many males. Effective religious leaders could satisfy this longing.

However, if boys and men see males in positions of authority in churches who are Abdicators or Fools, it makes it difficult for them to access their own heroic Sovereign or Seer energy. On the other hand, if their religious leaders have been Tyrants or Manipulators, men may need to do lengthy grieving over the slaying of their inner Sovereign by overbearing or underhanded pastors when they were children. This "slaughter of the innocents" through guilt, shame, and legalism may take a long time to heal.

However, if a man is still upset that his priest, minister, or pastor created shame in him, he has fallen into the trap of the Masochist, that is, victimhood. If he is in his fifties and still hurt by events from long ago, it is important for him to realize that it is only his own thoughts that are hurting him now, and it is possible to change his thinking. The turning point in accessing his own inner Sovereign and Seer may be for him to realize that the problem is no longer his pastor, but his own hurt feelings.

Although his pastor may have been operating mainly out of one of the antiheroic archetypes, the pastor also probably had the heroic archetypes working in him to some degree. Perhaps a man can start to focus on remembering some of his pastor's positive qualities such as the Lover's compassion, generosity, or great sense of humor. If his pastor was dysfunctional because of perfectionism, maybe the man needs to honor his pastor's human side. In any case, he needs a more balanced view of his pastor. Superhuman expectations are sure to cause disillusionment.

Beyond changing his own attitudes, perhaps a man can deal with his dysfunctional religious leader, if he is still living, either by confronting him face-to-face or by writing a letter. Or perhaps, rather than confronting his pastor, the wounded person can symbolically confront him through writing an angry letter he doesn't send, or through role-playing in a men's group such as the ManKind Project offers (see its Web site at www.mkp.org). The real turning point in these groups often happens when a man discovers that he is his own worst enemy, that he is projecting what he doesn't like or accept in himself onto others, and starts loving himself. Christ said, "Love your enemies, and pray for those who persecute you." Often, that is our own selves!

Every man, if he is to reconnect with the church, needs two rooms in his head for his pastor: a light room, in which he recognizes his pastor's strengths, and a dark room, in which he keeps cognizant of his pastor's human frailties. He can then let his real pastor into his soul, and let go of the overly ideal or overly imperfect pastor he has imagined his pastor to be, which in both cases causes disillusionment. Finally, after accepting his own projections onto his pastor, and after accepting his pastor as a real, flesh-and-blood human being, perhaps a man can let the church, and the idea of God acting through the church, back into his life.

If a man belongs to another major religious tradition, whether Jewish, Muslim, Hindu, or Buddhist, and has been wounded by male religious leaders, the same process would apply. No matter what the tradition, wisdom for men will consist in forgiving their male religious leaders for being human.

Chapter Nine

CONCLUSION

The basic idea of this book has been that the four main archetypes of Sovereign, Warrior, Seer, and Lover are spiritual heroes living within each human being, and that they have a profound impact upon the way men and women give spiritual guidance and direction. This impact can be either profoundly positive for the seeker or directee, if the spiritual guide is operating out of the heroic archetypes, or profoundly negative, if the spiritual director is under the influence of the antiheroic archetypes: the Tyrant, Abdicator, Sadist, Masochist, Manipulator, Fool, Addict, or Frigid.

This whole archetypal area that we have been investigating has great importance for the life of Christian and other religious communities and traditions, because every year so many people go to spiritual directors or guides with the hope of receiving sound guidance for their spiritual journey. While the impact of Carl Jung on spiritual direction has been felt through the widespread use of the Myers Briggs Type Indicator, which is based on Jung's personality theory, there has been, until now, no in-depth application to spiritual direction of Jung's deeper theory of the collective unconscious and its contents, that is, the archetypes.

We have seen in this book that the archetypes are extraordinarily powerful in ordering individual human behavior. They are so powerful that they have, in fact, shaped every human culture: the Sovereign, Warrior, Seer, and Lover archetypes are found in one form or another everywhere and in every age. They have profoundly influenced mythology, history, religion, and literature down through the centuries. This is because they are underlying patterns of behavior that are hardwired into the human psyche. Jung believes they are as elemental and essential to human behavior as instincts.

So, as with instincts, we can try to ignore the archetypes, but they are not going to go away. We are faced with the choice of either recognizing them, and thus being able to work with them to greatly enrich our lives, or we can ignore them and so fall under their unconscious control of our destinies. Archetypes that are ignored and not dealt with in a conscious, healthy way, will go underground and eventually erupt into our behavior in their Shadow form, with dire consequences. Therefore, it is imperative, when a person is as spiritually open and vulnerable as people tend to be in spiritual direction, that spiritual directors be aware of what archetypes are influencing their behavior.

SUMMARY OF THE IMPACT OF ARCHETYPES ON GUIDES AND SEEKERS

In the course of this book, we have examined extensive descriptions of the heroic and antiheroic versions of the Sovereign, Warrior, Seer, and Lover archetypes and then pondered how these ideal and anti-ideal descriptions would apply to spiritual guidance and direction. My intent has been to provide spiritual guides and directors a new standard of excellence to strive for, as well as a new awareness of foundational weaknesses they need to avoid. So to conclude, let us now sum all this up.

We have seen how the heroic Sovereign Director is centered and calm and benevolently authoritative (not authoritarian).

The Sovereign Director helps directees to have well-ordered and fertile spiritual lives that are rooted in the real world. Sovereign Directors are effusive in their blessing and praise of directees, and the love and protection of God flows through Sovereign Directors to their directees.

The impact on directees is that they have a new sense of security and safety in God. They feel rooted and grounded in God, so that passing troubles and turmoil no longer deeply disturb them. Their lives become centered on God and God's reign. Their priorities become reordered according to God's will. Rooted in reality and feeling blessed by God, they also feel empowered to reach out and be a blessing to all those around them.

The Tyrant Director on the other hand is authoritarian and insecure and dominates the directee. Tyrant Directors are para- noid about maintaining control of the spiritual direction session and secretly (or overtly) rage if they are not obeyed and adored by directees. Their putdowns are a curse for directees. Rather than feeling blessed, directees sense that any new life or spiritual growth in them is being blocked.

As an Abdicator Director, the Shadow Sovereign goes to the other extreme, losing all control of the spiritual direction ses- sion and abdicating any responsibility for the spiritual growth of directees. Abdicator Directors are absent, if not physically then mentally and emotionally, when directees need them the most.

The effect of a Tyrant Director on directees is to make them afraid of God and of life. They come to doubt the legitimacy of their own experiences of God, and to see God as a punishing rule-maker just waiting for someone to step outside the Law. Consequently, directees feel no sense of freedom or grace in their spiritual lives and are likely to become legalistic, guilt- ridden, and scrupulous, that is, overly obsessed with doing everything perfectly. They feel destroyed rather than renewed in their relationship with God.

With the Abdicator, the directee feels profoundly insecure, that God cannot be relied upon for aid in difficult situations. Directees lose all sense that God is watching over and guiding them. They feel profoundly disillusioned when Abdicator Directors abandon them when they are suffering.

Heroic Warrior Directors are alert to everything, every verbal and nonverbal nuance from both themselves and directees. Warrior Directors are wily tacticians of spiritual growth. Self-controlled and responsible, they take decisive action to help directees cut away anything, any religious habit or attitude, that no longer serves them. The Warrior Director is ready and willing to fight demons of chaos and sin wherever they have engulfed the directee. Warrior Directors are totally dedicated to wage long and hard war to achieve their transpersonal cause: the spiritual growth of their directees.

Directees working with Warrior Directors are empowered to confront, perhaps for the first time, what is genuinely working for them spiritually, and what is not. They become motivated to simplify their spiritual life, to keep what is fruitful, and to cut away unnecessary religious baggage. With the Warrior Director's help, directees are emboldened to face their demons, compulsions, addictions, sins, and temptations and to go the distance to overcome them.

Directees no longer feel overwhelmed by their main spiritual enemy, the Shadow within. With the help of the Warrior Director, directees have the courage to bring their Shadow to the light, admit the Shadow's power over them, and to disempower their Shadow by being aware of it and how it operates to sabotage their lives. For example, directees may be willing to admit for the first time that they are angry with God, and how this anger with God causes them to be cynical about everything. However, now that they can be honest about their anger, they can examine it to see if it makes any sense and no longer let it rule unconsciously over their spiritual life.

The Shadow Warrior Director, the Sadist, has a completely different agenda from the Warrior Director. The only cause of Sadist Directors is their own benefit, whether it is financial gain or the perverse delight they derive from causing directees pain. They are cruel, disparage the directees' spiritual experiences, destroy their enthusiasm, and insensitively violate their personal boundaries.

Masochist Directors, on the other hand, give too much power to directees. They let directees unjustly criticize them for not being conservative or liberal enough and allow directees to violate their boundaries, for example, letting directees call them at any hour, day or night.

The directee under a Sadist Director will feel totally devalued and worthless in the sight of God. As with the Tyrant, directees will feel that their spiritual experiences are invalid. They will learn to disparage the spiritual experiences of themselves and others and wonder if God causes suffering, wants us to suffer, and delights in our pain. In short, their image of God as torturer will fill them with doubt and guilt, and they will lose their enthusiasm for spirituality and religion. They will confuse God and the demonic more and more.

The impact of the Masochist Director, on the other hand, will be that directees will become spiritually proud, convinced that their narrow viewpoint is the only valid one and that spiritual guides will agree with anything they say. Directees will become more judgmental and less open to the fundamental human right of freedom of religion. The more narrow directees become, the more dangerous they are to the rest of society.

Heroic Seer Directors use their wisdom, gained from years of studying theology, scripture, ritual, and the mystics, as well as from experimenting continually with their own religious practices and methods, to serve, heal, and initiate directees into life-giving spirituality. The whole being of Seer Directors is aligned with the cosmic Way, the Logos, the Tao, the Christ. They are a direct bridge to the spiritual world and help directees to understand and access the eternal order underlying everything. They use both reason and intuition for the directee's benefit.

With the Seer Director, the directee will be in awe of the Seer's knowledge and wisdom and will come to understand just how much there is to learn in the spiritual life. Directees will experience a heightened interest in studying theology, scripture, and spirituality, and in trying out various religious disciplines and methods. They will feel healed of old spiritual, emotional, and sexual wounds and gain a new sense of liberation, empowerment, and holiness as they learn to align themselves with the Logos, the Spirit, and the Eternal Order.

Manipulator Directors (Shadow Seer Directors), on the other hand, use directees for their own ends. Like the Tyrant and the Sadist Directors, their goal is power over, not power with, directees. They use manipulation to make directees dependent on their secret knowledge, and then schedule extra, unnecessary sessions and charge high fees. Manipulator Directors can be either overly rational, and therefore not open to the subtle intuitive promptings of the Spirit, or they can abandon reason altogether and dissolve into New Age psychobabble, being so intuitive and spiritual that they lose their foothold in reality. They may falsely claim to have mystical powers such as the ability to forecast the directee's future, or they may use, for example, Tarot cards and astrology to mislead directees.

Fool Directors, on the other hand, gain power in a back-handed way by subtly sabotaging any attempt directees make to grow spiritually. The directees can never clearly identify what is happening, but they always have a feeling of being undermined by the Fool Director. Fool Directors are slippery, elusive, and passive-aggressive but deny any underlying hostile motives.

Under the spell of the Manipulator Director, directees lose any sense of freedom. They feel that they are not adults, but dependent children. They do not feel like they are in charge of their own process in spiritual direction, able to make their own decisions and come to their own solutions and conclusions regarding their spiritual life. The Manipulator Director tells directees what to do rather than asking them what *they* think they should do. If the Manipulator Director is overly rational or overly intuitive, the directee may become legalistic and rigid on the one hand, or unrealistic and confused on the other.

With the Fool Director, directees will feel profoundly uneasy without knowing why. Directees may be encouraged to take irrational risks, and when they fail, directees may lose trust in God and their own ability to discern God's will. They may stop praying and become disillusioned about religion and the spiritual life.

Heroic Lover Directors love directees with God's love. They are a direct channel of God's wisdom and grace. They mentor directees in living with passion, joy, enthusiasm, and playfulness. They teach directees to appreciate all aspects of God's creation, to revel in responsible sensuality and sexuality, to have compassion, and to engage in justice for Earth and all its creatures.

With the Lover Director, directees get a real, felt sense of just how good God's love is. As with the Sovereign Director, directees feel truly blessed and open their hearts, minds, souls, and spirits more and more to God. They learn to enjoy life and sensuality and to be playful on the one hand and, on the other hand, to be responsible, ethical, compassionate, and just.

Addict Directors are lost in sensuality. They put no boundaries on pleasure. They are spiritual gluttons, reveling in ecstatic experiences, both their own and those of directees, but they help no one. They are unable to commit themselves to companioning directees if directees are suffering, in desolation, or going through a lengthy dark night of the soul. There is always a danger of Addict Directors trying to get directees hooked on irresponsible sensuality, or of Addict Directors sexually abusing directees when they are most vulnerable.

The other Shadow polarity of the Lover archetype, when applied to spiritual direction, is the Frigid Director. Numbed out and with no warmth, Frigid Directors cannot help directees love themselves and others more or become more intimate with God. Frigid Directors are cynical, depressed, and burned out in their ministry, and therefore cannot adequately serve directees.

With Addict Directors, directees feel *too* free. Having no boundaries or commandments or religious laws creates a sense of lostness and deep anxiety. Ungrounded ecstasy and mysticism leave directees feeling unreal. On the other hand, when directees are suffering, they will feel profoundly betrayed if the Addict Director either abandons them or sexually abuses them when they are vulnerable.

With Frigid Directors, directees feel their own hearts begin to shut down. They lose their enthusiasm for God's ways and their love of self and others. They lose their vision for God's reign and feel more and more disconnected from God and their own soul.

How Seekers Can Cope with an Antiheroic Spiritual Guide

The directee who has a director working out of one or more of the antiheroic archetypes will naturally think of stopping spiritual direction. However, there can be many reasons why directees keep going with a dysfunctional director. For example, they may want to be in spiritual direction but don't know any other spiritual directors. They may live in an area where there are few directors or all the good directors are booked up. They may have a compassionate heart and want to give the director a second chance, or they may see redeeming qualities in the director and want to try to work out any difficulties. They may be required to be in spiritual direction as part of their training to be a spiritual director, or they may be on retreat and there are no other spiritual directors available. If any of these situations apply, directees could try the following coping strategies.

The best way to cope with a Tyrant Director, other than quitting, is with an assertive (not aggressive or passive-aggressive) show of your own strength. Show Tyrant Directors that you will stand up to them in a tactful way, without destroying their inner Abdicator, the insecure child within that Tyrants are trying to hide with their bluster. When we are assertive, we take care of both our needs and the needs of others.

Assert that God is your true Spiritual Director, and that you are first of all called by God to obey God's will and to submit to the Tyrant Director only if you believe that what the Tyrant is suggesting is in line with God's will. State that your God is first of all a God of freedom and grace, and only secondarily a god of laws and rules, and that you believe that your spiritual experiences are as valid as those of anyone.

With the Abdicator Director, keep reminding yourself that God is your absolutely loving and sovereign eternal protector and provider. Abdicators may abandon you when you need them the most, but God will always be there for you.

The best way for directees to cope with Sadist Directors is to let them know the impact of their actions on your feelings. Sadist Directors have no awareness of how they are making directees feel, since they are totally out of touch with their own feelings. Say something like, "When you ask questions that are too personal, I feel scared (or intimidated or violated) because it seems like you are not respecting my boundaries." In dealing with Masochist Directors, encourage them to honestly state their own beliefs and feelings, and then respect their right to religious beliefs different from yours. Also, respect their time and their energy boundaries. Going beyond the one-hour boundary in sessions or calling the Masochist Director for help outside of the sessions will not help you be focused or responsible for your own spiritual growth.

To cope with Manipulator Directors, expose their nefarious machinations to the light by saying something like, "When you do such and such, I feel manipulated" or "Are you trying to manipulate me?" or "I don't think I need to come for extra sessions." Fool Directors are much harder to pin down because they are more subtle and elusive than the Manipulators, but at least you could let them know that you are watching them closely by saying something like, "I feel uneasy about that. I don't know why, but I just feel uncomfortable," or "I think that what you are suggesting is too risky and could result in problems for me."

With the Addict or Frigid Director, directees can cope by exposing the addictive or frigid behavior in a nonjudgmental way. Addict and Frigid Directors may have no awareness of how they are coming across, so you may be doing them a favor and waking them up by pointing it out to them. Reassuring directors of your unconditional esteem for them may also give them the confidence and motivation to break out of their self-destructive ways. The directee might say something like, "Even though you do such and such, I think that is just maladaptive surface behavior. I see a wonderful, caring, and intelligent person behind all that, and I hope to see more of that in future spiritual direction sessions."

With all directors, as with all human beings, shaming them for bad behavior will probably just make them worse. Helping them see, or believe in, their nobility, their inner hero beneath the surface dysfunction, will motivate them to give spiritual direction in a more heroic way. People in general tend to become what we make them.

So the best way to cope with antiheroic directors in all cases is to tactfully confront or expose their negative behavior and call them to be accountable. They will probably not be aware of what they have been doing or of their impact on directees. They may thank you for your honesty, and be more than willing to try to correct their inappropriate behavior now that they are aware of it.

Of course, it is not the directee's responsibility to cure an antiheroic director, but directors might be given one or two second chances to mend their ways. If their dysfunctional behavior is pointed out several times, antiheroic directors will have been given fair warning that they will lose this directee if they do not change. Be aware that directors may not change permanently, but they may change long enough to meet the directee's needs.

If after several instances of calling the director to account the directee finds there is no significant improvement in the director's behavior, the directee should definitely break off the spiritual direction relationship. Directees might then want to contact Spiritual Directors International (the professional body that oversees spiritual directors worldwide; see its Web site at www.sdiworld.org) or its local spiritual directors association, which may be able to help them locate other directors in their area. There may be many more spiritual directors out there than the directee thinks. If directees know individuals who are receiving spiritual direction, they could ask them for their spiritual director's contact information. Finding a good local spiritual director may take some perseverance on the part of the directee.

There is also always the possibility of doing spiritual direction by long distance phone or e-mail, which are not as good as face-to-face spiritual direction but still can work well if they are the only options, the director is willing to do it, it is done prayerfully, and if the directee has a low-cost phone plan or the directee and director have access to e-mail.

In all the heroic cases of spiritual direction, God is both the Center and the true Director of the sessions. Directors, in their various archetypal manifestations, simply and humbly get their own ego out of the way and are there to do God's will and serve directees. Thus, tremendous spiritual growth of directees can happen. On the other hand, in both negative polarities of the various antiheroic directors, God is not allowed to be in charge. Either the director or the directee becomes the center and director of the sessions, and so no genuine spiritual growth takes place.

IMPLICATIONS OF ARCHETYPES FOR SPIRITUAL GUIDANCE AND PLANETARY SALVATION

As already stated, archetypal theory has profound implications for the field of spiritual direction. In chapter 8, we examined the many ways in which directees and spiritual directors can learn to access and activate the archetypes so that they can become more heroic. Directors can not only be much more cognizant of the Shadow side of the archetypes and be vigilant in defending themselves against their negative influence; they can also look to the positive archetypes for examples of the heroic spiritual director.

One implication of this is that archetypes give spiritual directors a standard or ideal to measure their own performance against. By familiarizing themselves with the ideal and most negative archetypal forms of the spiritual director, directors will be able to judge more accurately whether or not they are going about spiritual direction properly. The best way to avoid the antiheroic archetypes is to behave in tune with their heroic forms. Greater consciousness of the positive and negative archetypes could result in much more effective spiritual direction in general.

Another implication is that, as part of training to be spiritual directors, individuals should be given the opportunity to study archetypes and to try to discern which of the positive or negative ones they tend to operate out of. They could then try to avoid the negative and accentuate the positive, or if one positive archetype is predominant, they could try to compensate for this by developing the other positive archetypes so that they become well-balanced spiritual directors. It is possible, for example, to have too much Lover as a spiritual director, and not enough Sovereign, Warrior, or Seer. Similarly, established spiritual directors who are already practicing their craft, could study Jungian psychology and learn more about archetypes in order to be more aware of archetypal influences in their spiritual direction practice.

A third implication is that a thorough understanding of archetypes could be another major tool for the field of spiritual direction, perhaps as important as, or more important than, the Myers Briggs Type Indicator or the Enneagram have proven to be. Enneagram types such as the Power Person or Reformer or Intellectual or Caregiver may in fact just be subtypes of the Sovereign, Warrior, Seer, or Lover archetypes. In other words, Enneagram types may really just be archetypes, and it may be possible to subsume the whole Enneagram under archetypal theory.

In any case, the most important implication as far as archetypes and spiritual direction are concerned is to know how we can best protect trusting and vulnerable directees from the influence of antiheroic archetypes operating in the spiritual director as well as how we can bring about great spiritual growth in directees by empowering them with the help of the director's heroic archetypes. Knowing the heroic and antiheroic archetypes will also help spiritual directors know when spiritual heroism or antiheroism is growing in the directee. Directors will have a clearer vision of what the fully spiritual man or woman is like, and whether or not they are helping their directees move in that direction. Knowing the archetypes sets a new and ideal standard not just for directors, but also for directees.

The whole thrust of evolution, as outlined in chapter 1, is in a spiritual direction from matter to life to thought to spirit. Evolution has already pressed beyond the geosphere (water and rocks) to the biosphere (plants and animals), and beyond that to the noosphere (thought), the sphere of the human mind. The spiritual growth and renewal of individual directees, individual churches, Christianity in general, and other world religions, will play a vital role in bringing the whole human race to the next stage in planetary evolution, the theosphere (spirit), that is, the reign of God.

The human race at this point in its evolutionary history is either going to learn how to love one another and God's creation, or we are going to destroy each other and our only homeland, that is, planet Earth.

Spiritual direction has the capability to help humanity move away from materialism and consumerism and find a truly human and proper spiritual path at this critical juncture. Knowledge of the heroic and antiheroic archetypes can play a key role in enabling spiritual directors to fill the world with mystics and bring the reign of the Supreme Sovereign, Warrior, Seer, and Lover to fruition.

Let me conclude by challenging all spiritual guides and directors and all spiritual seekers and directees to become more heroic, with these words of Joseph Campbell from *The Hero with a Thousand Faces:*

> The heroes of all times have gone before us. The labyrinth is thoroughly known. We have only to follow the thread of the hero path. And where we had thought to find an abomination, we shall find God. And where we had thought to slay another, we shall slay ourselves. Where we had thought to travel outward, we will come to the center of our own existence. And where we had thought to be alone, we will be with all the world.

NOTES

Chapter One: Introduction

1. Joseph Campbell, *The Power of Myth* (New York: Doubleday, 1988), 51.
2. Carl Gustav Jung, *The Collected Works of C. G. Jung*, vol. 9, part 1: *The Archetypes and the Collective Unconscious* (Princeton, NJ: Princeton University Press, 1959), 39.
3. Robert Moore and Douglas Gillette, *King, Warrior, Magician, Lover: Rediscovering the Archetypes of the Mature Masculine* (San Francisco: HarperCollins, 1990), xi.
4. Ibid., xvii.
5. Ibid., 16–17.
6. Ibid., 71.

Chapter Two: The Nature of Archetypes

1. Jung, *Collected Works: The Archetypes*, 43.
2. Ibid., 44.
3. Ibid., 4.
4. Moore and Gillette, *King, Warrior, Magician, Lover*, 44.
5. Jung, *Collected Works: The Archetypes*, 69.
6. Ibid., 157.
7. Jolande Jacobi, *The Psychology of C. G. Jung*, 7th ed.(New Haven: Yale University Press, 1968), 50.
8. Carol Pearson, *Awakening the Heroes Within: Twelve Archetypes to Help Us Find Ourselves and Transform Our World* (San Francisco: Harper, 1991), 5–6.
9. Tad and Noreen Guzie, *About Men and Women: How Your Masculine and Feminine Archetypes Shape Your Destiny* (New York: Paulist Press, 1986), 7–8.
10. Ibid., 132.
11. Jung, *Collected Works: The Archetypes*, 7–8.
12. Ibid., 13.

Chapter Three: In Defense of the Warrior and Sovereign

1. Patrick Arnold, *Wildmen, Warriors, and Kings: Masculine Spirituality and the Bible* (New York: Crossroad, 1991), 101.
2. Robert Bly, *Iron John: A Book about Men* (Reading, MA: Addison-Wesley, 1990), 165.
3. Moore and Gillette, *King, Warrior, Magician, Lover,* 78.
4. Ibid., 79.
5. Bly, *Iron John,* 159.
6. Cited in Moore and Gillette, *King, Warrior, Magician, Lover,* 76.
7. Bly, *Iron John,* 179.
8. Ibid., 168.
9. Moore and Gillette, *King, Warrior, Magician, Lover,* xix.
10. Max Oliva, *The Masculine Spirit: Resources for Reflective Living* (Notre Dame, IN: Ave Maria Press, 1977), 9.

Chapter Four: The Heroic Sovereign, Warrior, Seer, and Lover

1. Arnold, *Wildmen, Warriors, and Kings,* 38.
2. Bly, *Iron John,* 108.
3. Moore and Gillette, *King, Warrior, Magician, Lover,* 52.
4. Ibid., 52–60.
5. Arnold, *Wildmen, Warriors, and Kings,* 114.
6. Pearson, *Awakening the Heroes Within,* 181–82.
7. Ibid., 183.
8. Oliva, *The Masculine Spirit,* 67.
9. Pearson, *Awakening the Heroes Within,* 94.
10. Moore and Gillette, *King, Warrior, Magician, Lover,* 83.
11. Pearson, *Awakening the Heroes Within,* 102.
12. Campbell, *The Power of Myth,* 132.
13. Pearson, *Awakening the Heroes Within,* 193.
14. Moore and Gillette, *King, Warrior, Magician, Lover,* 102.
15. Oliva, *The Masculine Spirit,* 73.
16. Pearson, *Awakening the Heroes Within,* 197.
17. Moore and Gillette, *King, Warrior, Magician, Lover,* 108.
18. Ibid., 118.
19. Oliva, *The Masculine Spirit,* 85.
20. Pearson, *Awakening the Heroes Within,* 204.
21. Oliva, *The Masculine Spirit,* 89.
22. Pearson, *Awakening the Heroes Within,* 148.
23. Arnold, *Wildmen, Warriors, and Kings,* 168.
24. Moore and Gillette, *King, Warrior, Magician, Lover,* 140.

Chapter Five: The Antiheroic Sovereign, Warrior, Seer, and Lover

1. Jacobi, *The Psychology of C. G. Jung*, 114.
2. Jung, *Collected Works: The Archetypes*, 39.
3. Arnold, *Wildmen, Warriors, and Kings*, 100.
4. Moore and Gillette, *King, Warrior, Magician, Lover*, 71–72.
5. Pearson, *Awakening the Heroes Within*, 187.
6. Ibid., 188.
7. Moore and Gillette, *King, Warrior, Magician, Lover*, 50.
8. Bly, *Iron John*, 171–72.
9. Moore and Gillette, *King, Warrior, Magician, Lover*, 141–42.
10. Oliva, *The Masculine Spirit*, 102–9.
11. Pearson, *Awakening the Heroes Within*, 155–56.

Chapter Eight: Becoming a Heroic Guide or Seeker

1. Moore and Gillette, *King, Warrior, Magician, Lover*, 145.
2. Ibid., 145–55.
3. Ibid., 149.
4. Pearson, *Awakening the Heroes Within*, 291.
5. Ibid., 294.
6. Arnold, *Wildmen, Warriors, and Kings*, 176.

RECOMMENDED READING

Arnold, Patrick. *Wildmen, Warriors, and Kings: Masculine Spirituality and the Bible.* New York: Crossroad, 1991.

Ball, Pamela. *10,000 Dreams Interpreted.* London: Arcturus Publishing, 1996.

Becker, Ernest. *The Denial of Death.* New York: Macmillan, 1990.

Bolen, Jean S. *Gods in Everyman: A New Psychology of Men's Lives and Loves.* San Francisco: Harper and Row, 1989.

Bly, Robert. *Iron John: A Book about Men.* Reading, MA: Addison-Wesley, 1990.

Brewi, Janice, and Anne Brennan. *Celebrate Mid-Life: Jungian Archetypes and Mid-Life Spirituality.* New York: Crossroad, 1993.

Campbell, Joseph. *The Hero with a Thousand Faces.* New York: Pantheon Books, 1949.

———. *The Power of Myth.* New York: Doubleday, 1988.

Conn, Joann Wolski. *Women's Spirituality.* New York: Paulist, 1986.

Conroy, Maureen. *Looking into the Well: Supervision of Spiritual Directors.* Chicago: Loyola, 1995.

Crosby, Michael. *Spirituality of the Beatitudes.* Maryknoll, NY: Orbis Books, 1981.

Downing, Christine, ed. *Mirrors of the Self: Archetypal Images That Shape Your Life.* Los Angeles: Tarcher, 1991.

Fischer, Kathleen. *Women at the Well: Feminist Perspectives on Spiritual Direction.* New York: Paulist, 1988.

Goldbrunner, Josef. *Individuation: A Study of the Depth Psychology of Carl Gustav Jung.* Notre Dame, IN: Notre Dame University Press, 1964.

Grosse, Frederick. *The Eight Masks of Men: A Practical Guide in Spiritual Growth for Men of the Christian Faith.* New York: Haworth Pastoral Press, 1998.

Guzie, Tad, and Guzie, Noreen. *About Men and Women: How Your Masculine and Feminine Archetypes Shape Your Destiny.* New York: Paulist, 1986.

Hagan, Kay Leigh, ed. *Women Respond to the Men's Movement.* San Francisco: HarperSanFrancisco, 1992.

Hall, Calvin, and Vernon Nordby. *A Primer of Jungian Psychology.* New York: Meridian, 1973.

Jacobi, Jolande. *The Psychology of C. G. Jung.* 7th ed. New Haven: Yale University Press, 1968.

Johnson, Robert. *Inner Work.* Harper and Row, 1986.

Jung, Carl Gustav. *Aspects of the Masculine.* Trans. R. F. C. Hull. Princeton University Press, 1989.

———. *The Collected Works of C. G. Jung.* Vol. 9, part 1: *The Archetypes and the Collective Unconscious.* Princeton, NJ: Princeton University Press, 1959.

Keen, Sam. *Fire in the Belly: On Being a Man.* New York: Bantam Books, 1991.

Kipnis, Aaron. *Knights without Armour: A Practical Guide for Men in Quest of the Masculine Soul.* New York: Putnam, 1991.

Lauter, Estella, and Carol Rupprecht, eds. *Feminist Archetypal Theory: Interdisciplinary Revisions of Jungian Thought.* Knoxville: University of Tennessee Press, 1985.

Leddy, Mary Jo. *Radical Gratitude.* Maryknoll, NY: Orbis Books, 2002.

Levant, Ronald, and William Pollack, eds. *A New Psychology of Men.* New York: Basic Books, 1995.

Mazis, Glen A. *The Trickster, Magician and Grieving Man: Reconnecting Men with Earth.* Santa Fe, NM: Bear and Co., 1993.

Moore, Robert, and Douglas Gillette. *King, Warrior, Magician, Lover: Rediscovering the Archetypes of the Mature Masculine.* San Francisco: HarperCollins, 1990.

———. *The King Within: Accessing the King in the Male Psyche.* New York: Avon, 1992.

———. *The Lover Within: Accessing the Lover in the Male Psyche.* New York: Morrow, 1993.

———. *The Magician Within: Accessing the Shaman in the Male Psyche.* New York: Morrow, 1993.

———. *The Warrior Within: Accessing the Knight in the Male Psyche.* New York: Morrow, 1992.

Myss, Caroline. *Sacred Contracts: Awakening Your Divine Potential.* New York: Harmony Books, 2001.

Oliva, Max. *The Masculine Spirit: Resources for Reflective Living.* Notre Dame, IN: Ave Maria Press, 1997.

Pable, Martin. *The Quest for the Male Soul: In Search of Something More.* Notre Dame, IN: Ave Maria Press, 1996.

Pearson, Carol. *Awakening the Heroes Within: Twelve Archetypes to Help Us Find Ourselves and Transform Our World.* San Francisco: Harper, 1991.

———. *The Hero Within: Six Archetypes We Live By.* 3rd ed. Harper-SanFrancisco, 1998.

Rohr, Richard. *Men and Women.* Audiotapes. Cincinnati: St. Anthony Messenger Press, 1999.

Schwartz-Salant, Nathan. *Archetypal Processes in Psychotherapy.* Wilmette, IL: Chiron, 1987.

Steinberg, Warren. *Masculinity: Identity, Conflict and Transformation.* Boston: Shambhala, 1993.

Tacey, David. *Remaking Men: Jung, Spirituality and Social Change.* New York: Routledge, 1997.

Teilhard de Chardin, Pierre. *The Phenomenon of Man.* London: Wm. Collins, 1955.

Turner, Trevor. "I Shop, Therefore I Am," *New Internationalist,* April 2003.

Ulanov, Ann. *The Healing Imagination: The Meeting of Psyche and Soul.* Einsiedeln, Switzerland: Daimon, 2000.

———. *Picturing God.* 2d rev. ed. Einsiedeln, Switzerland: Daimon, 2002.

———. *Receiving Woman: Studies in the Psychology and Theology of the Feminine.* Philadelphia: Westminster Press, 1981.

———. *Spiritual Aspects of Clinical Work.* Einsiedeln, Switzerland: Daimon, 2004.

Ulanov, Ann, and Ulanov, Barry. *Primary Speech: A Psychology of Prayer.* Louisville, KY: John Knox Press, 1982.

Wauters, Ambika. *Chakras and Their Archetypes: Uniting Energy Awareness and Spiritual Growth.* Freedom, CA: Crossing Press, 1977.

Whitehead, James, and Evelyn Whitehead. *Shadows of the Heart: A Spirituality of the Negative Emotions.* New York: Crossroad, 1994.